Assessment Centres

Assessment Centres

A Practical Handbook

Paul Jansen

and

Ferry de Jongh

Briar Hill Consult, Zoetermeer, The Netherlands

JOHN WILEY & SONS

Chichester · New York · Brisbane · Toronto · Singapore

Copyright © 1997 by Uitgeverij Het Spectrum B.V.
Published by John Wiley & Sons Ltd,
      Baffins Lane, Chichester,
      West Sussex PO19 1UD, England

      National   01243 779777
      International (+44) 1243 779777
      e-mail (for orders and customer service enquiries):
      cs-books@wiley.co.uk
      Visit our Home Page on http://www.wiley.co.uk
            or http://www.wiley.com

Previously published 1993 by Het Spectrum B.V. under the title:
Assessment Centers een open boek

Other Wiley Editorial Offices

John Wiley & Sons, Inc., 605 Third Avenue,
New York, NY 10158-0012, USA

Jacaranda Wiley Ltd, 33 Park Road, Milton,
Queensland 4064, Australia

John Wiley & Sons (Canada) Ltd, 22 Worcester Road,
Rexdale, Ontario M9W 1L1, Canada

John Wiley & Sons (Asia) Pte Ltd, 2 Clementi Loop #02-01,
Jin Xing Distripark, Singapore 129809

Library of Congress Cataloging-in-Publication Data

Jansen, Paulus Gerardus Wilhelmus. 1954–
    [Assessment centers. English]
    Assessment centers : a practical handbook / Paul Jansen and Ferry
De Jongh.
      p. cm.
    Includes bibliographical references and index.
    ISBN 0-471-96451-4 (pbk)
    1. Assessment centers (Personnel management procedure)   I. Jongh,
Ferry de. II. Title.
HF5549.5.A78J36   1997
658.3'14—dc20
                                                96–44892
                                                  CIP

British Library Cataloguing in Publication Data

A catalogue record for this book is available from the British Library

ISBN 0–471–964514

Typeset in 11/13pt Palatino from the author's disks by Dorwyn Ltd,
Rowlands Castle, Hants
Printed and bound in Great Britain by Biddles Ltd, Guildford and King's Lynn
This book is printed on acid-free paper responsibly manufactured from sustainable
forestation, for which at least two trees are planted for each one used for paper
production.

Contents

PART 5   EVALUATION OF THE ASSESSMENT CENTRE

Preface

An Assessment Centre is an evaluation process which can be used to identify the potential of employees and job candidates for a broad range of functions. Even though an increasing number of organisations use Assessment Centres ("AC"), little has been written on the subject that is suited for practitioners. Indeed it was not until the 1990s that such "practical" publications began to appear (see the end of this book). This has forced users to reinvent the wheel and engage in a process which involves a lot of trial and error. This process can and should be avoided. This is what we have set out to achieve in this book. "Assessment Centres" provides readers with an inside view of ACs and a clear and comprehensive idea of how to put an AC into practice. It should make ACs far more accessible than before.

Assessment Centres is a practical handbook. Theoretical discourses have been kept to a minimum. The reader will find numerous examples of procedures, diagrams, questionnaires, practical suggestions and pitfalls. The contributors have a great deal of experience with ACs and work for various organisations who are active in this area. They have attempted to keep nothing secret. Their texts are based on first-hand knowledge and contain detailed descriptions of every stage in the AC process, from planning to evaluation.

After a general introduction in Part 1, the basic principles of ACs are dealt with in Part 2. Chapter 2 looks at the way in which "dimensions" are used to classify and identify different types of behaviour. Chapter 3 looks at the assignments on which the candidates are tested. Chapter 4 deals with "assessors". Assessors are managers who have been trained to assess candidates in an AC. The development side of an AC is dealt with in Chapter 5.

xiv _____ Preface

Part 3 focuses on the various aspects of the AC sessions. Chapter 6 looks at role-players and their task of eliciting concrete behaviour. Chapter 7 looks at how assignments are recorded and evaluated. Chapters 8 and 9 deal with the management side of the AC. Chapter 8 looks at the director's role and Chapter 9 examines the logistic side of ACs.

Part 4 focuses on how to conclude the AC. Chapter 10 looks at AC reports. Chapter 11 deals with the assessment interview. During this candidates discuss the AC report with an advisor. Chapter 12 looks at aftercare in the form of follow-up activities to the AC.

Part 5 focuses on the appraisal of an AC. Chapter 13 looks at the way in which candidates, assessors and the contractor are asked to evaluate ACs. Chapter 14 examines the predictive validity of ACs and their financial returns. Chapter 15 looks at ways in which ACs can be used for management development within organisations and discusses the importance of integrating ACs in personnel assessment and development policies.

Finally, we would like to thank Louise van den Berk for her editorial assistance.

Paul Jansen
Ferry De Jongh

PART 1

General Introduction to the Assessment Centre

_____ Chapter 1

What is an Assessment Centre?

J. Seegers

1.1 INTRODUCTION

The term Assessment Centre may suggest a specific building or institute, or some form of training. However, it has nothing to do with these. An Assessment Centre is an evaluation process which can be used to identify the future potential of employees and job candidates.

Over the past few years, the Assessment Centre method has become increasingly popular. It consists of the observation of candidates carrying out a variety of assignments, individually or in a group, over a period of several days. The method is systematic, effective and reliable. It is designed to enable personnel officers, career advisors and especially line managers, to determine which qualities are essential for successful job performance, to evaluate people and identify future potential.

The term "Assessment Centre" (AC) is used in four contexts:

- The Assessment Centre technique as it is used in simulations and role play.

Assessment Centres: A Practical Handbook, P. Jansen and F. de Jongh.
© 1997 John Wiley & Sons Ltd.

- The Assessment Centre programme which is designed for selection, assessment and training purposes (in this case the AC does not only contain simulations and role plays but also other selection techniques such as psychological tests and interviews).
- Assessment Centre sessions during which the actual evaluation of a candidate takes place.
- Assessment Centre technology, or principles of the Assessment Centre method used as a basis for dealing with personnel issues.

The following elements are central to the Assessment Centre method:

- First and foremost, present behaviour can be used to predict future behaviour.
- For the assessment of job suitability reference is made to a set of carefully formulated criteria which are based on the results of a precise job analysis.
- The various assignments are geared towards the demands of a future job and often include reconstructions of situations that the job would entail known as "simulations".
- Group assignments can be used to observe how candidates deal with one another.
- More than one assessor is employed in the assessment process. Assessors are preferably managers who have more authority than those under assessment.
- The final result is based on the outcome of various assessments.

1.2 A SHORT HISTORY OF THE ASSESSMENT CENTRE

The Assessment Centre method is based on selection techniques which were used at the beginning of the 20th Century. However, it was not until the 1970s that substantial developments took place.

After the First World War, Germany decided to build a new army which would be far stronger than any before. Large scale reorganisations took place. Selection procedures and training schemes were introduced. They were the first of their kind to include practical assignments.

Although their methodology was highly criticised, German Assessment Centres were in fact used as a basis for British and American Assessment Centre programmes. The British War Office Selection Board, for example, adopted German selection methods. At roughly the same time, the Office of Strategic Services in the United States started to apply the German method to its selection procedure for secret agents and secretaries.

As for industry, the Assessment Centre method was first used by the American Telephone and Telegraph Company (AT&T) in the United States. In 1956 AT&T started a programme known as The Management Progress Study. It represents one of the most important developments in the Assessment Centre method. In the assessment programme set up by AT&T, candidates took part in group assignments, simulations, interviews and tests. Each candidate was assessed on 25 criteria. The results were used to predict the candidate's chances of being promoted to a middle management function within a period of ten years. The results of the AT&T programme were never disclosed to the candidates (or to management for that matter). Every year candidates were interviewed and their progress evaluated. After eight years a second assessment took place; after twenty years service, a third. Thirty years later, the programme is still running.

Standard Oil was the first organisation to copy AT&T's example, followed by IBM and General Electric. In 1969 thirteen organisations used programmes similar to that of AT&T. The aim of these programmes was initially selection. Later the Assessment Centre method was used to identify potential for the purposes of management development, career development and training.

The Equal Employment Opportunity Committee (EEOC) which was established in 1978, is an organisation which campaigns for equal rights for minorities in the United States and has had a very positive influence on the use of the Assessment Centre-method in that country. Over the last twenty years, the Assessment Center-method has started to gain more interest from countries outside the United States and Canada. Today, this method is being used by Japanese, Australian, South African and countless West European companies, including British Post Office, British Airways, ICL, Mars, Merck-Sharp & Dohme, Heineken, Siemens, NCR, Royal Dutch Airlines, Rank Xerox, IBM and Shell (see also section 1.5).

1.3   THE ASSESSMENT CENTRE AND OTHER TECHNIQUES

Many of the methods that are used during selection or promotion procedures try to assess whether candidates are suitable for a new function by observing their behaviour and assessing their performance in previous jobs. This can only be effective if the new job does not differ too much from the previous one, otherwise prediction of future performance can be precarious.

An excellent salesman, for example, won't necessarily be a good sales manager. It is important for a salesman to be able to sell. This requires an ability to organise work and naturally a flair for selling. A sales manager, however, has to ensure that his sales personnel are able to conduct the business of selling. Furthermore, a sales manager should be able to plan, organise and delegate work and place things in a broader context. A salesman would have no experience of these types of responsibilities, so it would be very difficult to assess job suitability based on his/her performance in previous jobs. The newly-appointed sales manager who was selected in this way would probably revert back to selling, instead of delegating tasks among his sales personnel. As for the company, it would still be in need of a sales manager and burdened with an overpaid salesman.

Even though jobs share the same targets, in this case sales, the higher their position in the job scale, the greater the difference in the type of demands that the job will involve. Technical skills, which are predominant in the lower levels, become virtually irrelevant at higher levels, whereas managerial skills become increasingly important. Further up in the job scale, management skills have broader terms of reference, as we see in Figure 1.1.

The Assessment Centre method can be used in cases like the one above, where candidates are being screened for jobs that they have no former experience of. Like psychological tests, the Assessment Centre method is an ideal way of assessing potential. However, it should not be seen as a replacement for the other techniques that are often used in selection procedures, such as interviews, psychological tests and job evaluations, but as a supplement to all these methods. If it is used to denote a programme the AC can even encompass such methods. Used in this way, the Assessment Centre can give companies a comprehensive idea of the capacities of (future) employees.

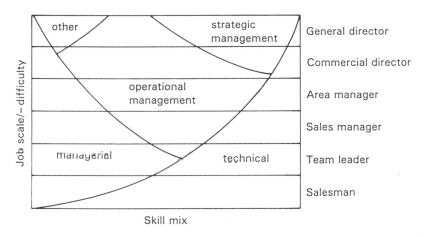

Figure 1.1 Job demands across the job scale: salesmen only require technical skills whereas team leaders need managerial skills as well as technical know-how

It is important to realise that Assessment Centre results are based on a candidate's performance at a certain time. Although they can provide a good indication of a candidate's future potential, they can never guarantee absolute certainty. The Assessment Centre method cannot provide completely airtight predictions, but does come very near to achieving this when used in combination with comprehensive selection techniques. The Assessment Centre results should, therefore, always be combined with information gathered from interviews, psychological tests and job evaluations. Medical records and interviews based on technical know-how would also be used in the case of external candidates. Indeed, the entire process of gathering information is often denoted as an "Assessment Centre".

During assessment procedures, we should always remember that a chain is only as strong as its weakest link. In the case of

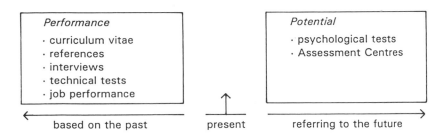

Figure 1.2 The Assessment Centre as part of an entire process

promotion, for example, candidates are often put forward by their head of department. These recommendations are often very subjective, prompted by a vague inkling, or personal preference, or even based on a "nice face". Candidates who are selected in this way often prove to be disappointing.

Another common mistake is to compare reliable results gained from thorough assessment techniques, with vague information gathered from past assessments or ineffective interviews. For example, a candidate will have a series of separate interviews with various company members such as a personnel officer, his prospective boss, another prospective superior and a colleague. All these different interviews tend to focus upon the same types of questions. No notes are made during interviews, giving free rein to personal interpretations. Furthermore, each selector looks at more or less the same criteria, for the simple reason that an interview is restricted to certain criteria; power of persuasion and manner, for example. If the various interviewers are more or less in agreement about the impressions they formed of a candidate, they will not send him/her for a psychological test. Often this is only found necessary when assessors can not reach an agreement, or have serious doubts about a candidate. In these cases a psychologist will be presented with a vague list of criteria on which the candidate is tested. To make matters worse these criteria often have no relevance to the criteria on which the psychological tests are based.

Reliable selection and promotion procedures can only be achieved by basing criteria upon the demands of a job. In this system, each assessment method should contribute to the total evaluation. Table 1.1 gives us an example of such a programme. Only one general interview is used in this procedure; the rest of the interviews have been replaced by other types of assessment methods. These methods do not involve more time than the interviews.

Since these methods are based upon specific criteria the results of each test contribute far more information to the total assessment. Assessment assignments provide information about other types of criteria. When setting up an assessment system like this, it is essential that each of the criteria is dealt with more than once, and that different people should be allowed to express their opinions. The discussion of conflicting opinions renders the system inclusive and ultimately reinforces its effectiveness. A well-functioning selection/promotion system

Table 1.1 Example of a selection or evaluation programme

Methods criteria	Structured general interview	Criterion orientated interview	Dialogue	In-basket + interview	Psycho-logical test
Biographical criteria	X				X
(Technical) training	X				X
Work experience	X				X
Technical know-how	X				
Planning and organising			(X)	X	
Delegating				X	
Problem analysis			X	X	X
Judgement			X	X	X
Powers of persuasion	(X)		X		
Ability to listen to others	X		X		X
Flexibility		X	X		X
Cooperation		X			X
Stress immunity			X	X	X
Performance motivation		X		X	X
Initiative		X	X	X	
Time	1 hr	1 hr dependent on no. of criteria	0.5 hr	2 hr	Dependent on no. of tests and if with/ without psychologist's interview

X: is measured using this technique
(X): can be measured using this technique

should consist of clearly-defined criteria and assessment stages, as well as expert assessors. Assessors should be trained in assessing people and preferably employed by the same organisation that is carrying out the selection procedure. Interviewers should be well-practised in criterion-orientated interviewing, and receive as much information as possible that is relevant to the specific criteria of the job.

Candidates are assessed throughout the sessions on various criteria. It is not until the various results have been correlated that a total picture of the candidate is formed. This stage of the evaluation process can be carried out by a selector or a selection team. The latter is preferable since it forces individual selectors to defend their own arguments and conclusions.

1.4   THE ASSESSMENT CENTRE IN STAGES

There are few companies whose use of the Assessment Centre method would be incidental, for the AC presupposes certain

Setting up an Assessment Centre: a step by step approach

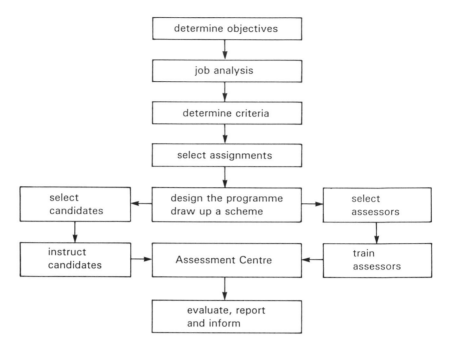

Figure 1.3 Step by step implementation of the Assessment Centre method

views about assessment and can be used for a wide range of purposes (selection, promotion, gauging of training requirements etc). It can become fully integrated, taking its place alongside other management tools (see Chapter 15). This integration should be carried out in various stages (see Figure 1.3).

Stage 1: Making an Inventory

At this stage the organisation should determine its target group, the aims of the assessment project and the desired results.

An analysis should comprise how the various jobs are constructed, why they exist, what sort of areas they affect, the responsibilities they entail, how they are evaluated, how performance is rewarded and what sort of future changes may take place (see Chapter 5). The situations that the job involves, critical situations in particular, play an essential role in this analysis. They determine the focus for the discussion of criteria and the choice of simulations. At this stage one should not rely solely on assessors, but refer to as many people as possible involved in the decision-making. The results of the analysis are included in a report. The final criteria should be determined by the organisation's management.

It is not always a good idea to restrict job analysis to a small circle of employees. This approach probably saves time, but may result in the omission of relevant points of view. It may not be common practice, but it would be useful to know what sort of expectations a *client* may have of an employee. In the case of a salesman, for example, making a good impression might be regarded as a relevant criterion. It should, however, be seen in relation to the customer and not to the impressions a salesman makes on his colleagues or superiors.

The main aim of selection procedures is to predict how someone will function in a new job. To do this it is essential to know the job inside out and determine what types of behaviour a candidate should demonstrate in order to carry out the job successfully. When the types of behaviour have been determined they should then be organised into categories so that they can be easily measured and interpreted during the selection process. During criterion-orientated interviews these categories are known as "criteria".

The difference between the "criteria" which a candidate requires in order to carry out a job, and the "specific requirements" that the candidate needs to comply with, can be rather confusing. "Criteria" specify an organisation's expectations of a candidate in terms of behaviour, whereas many so-called job requirements only refer indirectly to a criterion. For example, organisations that only require candidates from academic backgrounds not only have a preference for academic titles but are more especially interested in criteria such as "learning capacity" or "specialised knowledge" (see Chapter 2). The fact that a candidate has an academic title provides us with information that can be relevant to this criteria, but nothing more than that. In sales jobs, organisations are not concerned about how much experience a candidate has, but if he/she can sell. Sales experience is not automatic proof that a candidate can sell. We can conclude that job requirements should only be used if they are indispensable or if they are needed to restrict the number of applicants. Criteria should be used as much as possible in job descriptions.

There are many reasons why the term criteria is preferential to terms such as characteristics, skills and capacities. First, the term "criteria" is more general, embracing skills, characteristics and so forth, which also makes it a more neutral term than others. Secondly, the term "criteria" does not presuppose value judgements and suggest something positive like capacity, for instance. In some cases it is better that a candidate does not have too much of a certain characteristic. If someone is too immune to stress, for example, that can easily lead to indifference. Finally, a list of criteria is not a list of virtues: it is nice if a candidate is socially-minded but this admirable quality may not be relevant to the job in question. Figure 1.4 shows how the criteria for behaviour and job requirements are determined. The job is divided into tasks (job description); different types of criteria are derived from these (job analysis); and then different assessment techniques are adapted to these criteria.

To summarise the main points involved in a job analysis:

- The method which is used to analyse the job and determine the criteria should be carefully worked out.
- Job analysis and the determining of criteria should have a set place in selection and evaluation procedures.
- The criteria should be clearly defined.
- An objective and verifiable method should be used to organise criteria in order of importance.

The methods which are normally used in job analysis do not meet these requirements.

The reason for this is that they set out to achieve other aims, like job classification and remuneration, job analysis and organisation analysis. Candidate profiles are often drawn up in a fairly global way, based on assumptions like, "we want the right man for the job".

The Assessment Centre and every other type of selection or promotion procedure loses its effectiveness if the job is not thoroughly analysed. Rushing into assessment without sufficient preparation leads to assessors not knowing what to look for during the actual sessions and, far worse, not knowing how to evaluate what they have observed. In this way the Assessment Centre will not provide the desired results.

Job analysis is not a one-off exercise. Both the job, the organisation and the environment in which the employee will work are constantly changing. So why is it that job profiles hardly ever change? In almost all cases, assessment criteria should be modified from time to time. An inaccurate job analysis can lead to

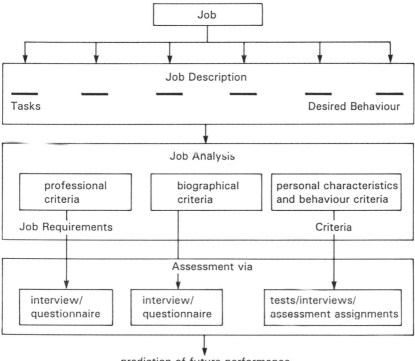

Figure 1.4 Determining criteria and job requirements

misleading evaluations, in which some criteria are assessed and other important criteria omitted. This renders the various evaluation methods ineffective.

Stage 2: Making the AC Operational

The Assessment Centre should be developed at this stage. This involves converting information acquired in phase 1 into assessment assignments, interviews and tests. These should be designed so that all the different criteria receive as much attention as possible. This phase involves mainly specialist activities. The final programme is then discussed with the employees that are involved in the selection/promotion procedures. Then the assessors are trained.

There are two training programmes, a shorter one consisting of two or three days and a longer version consisting of four to five days. A two to three day training programme should be seen as the absolute minimum, and for many reasons is not preferable. A programme like this is more of a crash course and provides insufficient preparation for an assessor to carry out his task effectively (see Chapter 4). It offers a quick look at a limited number of assignments but there is no time to deal with the essential aspects of the assessment process. If someone does opt for the shorter programme he/she should have sufficient "on the job" experience also (see Chapter 14).

The types of assignments used in an Assessment Centre should imitate aspects and situations that the job would entail. Because the assignments are intended to stimulate job-related behaviour, they should resemble the actual work; be of the same nature and have the same level of complexity as the work itself. Criteria should be very carefully determined and should contain all the elements that are common and essential to the job. The actual assignments should imitate the most usual and essential task aspects. They should be constructed so that they stimulate relevant, concrete behaviour that can be easily observed and assessed.

The development of effective assignments and simulations which comply with these demands is complicated and time-consuming. Often, assignments are used which do not stimulate job-related behaviour. It is not only a task that should be reconstructed, but also a situation (see Chapter 2). Another important consideration is the number of people involved in the assignments. A group assignment, for example, should only be included if working in a group is an essential part of the job. A group assignment would not be an obvious choice for managerial staff, since managers are more involved in individual relations than group activities.

A common mistake is to make assignments either too difficult or too easy. An assignment's level of complexity should correspond with the job. The criterion "planning and organising" is important for a sales director as well as a sales representative. The sales representative, however, only has to plan and organise his visits, whereas the sales director has to formulate strategic plans and set priorities for himself and others. This difference should be expressed in the assignments. Furthermore, assignments should be designed so that internal candidates or candidates with prior experience do not have an unfair advantage over others.

Stage 3: Implementation

A scheme is made which states who has to do what where. The assessors, the "directors" (see Chapter 8) and role-players as well as the candidates are given a copy of this.

An ideal standard for assessment sessions is one to two days per every six to eight participants, three or four assessors and at least three or four role-players, all depending on the size of the programme.

Stage 4: Evaluation

A report is written, then candidates are told their results. This can be done by a psychologist or one of the assessors.

When everything is completed, the programme should be evaluated and any necessary changes made (see Chapter 13).

1.5   ASSESSMENT CENTERS IN PRACTICE

The use of the Assessment Centre method has increased rapidly over the past decades. Out of all the first versions of the Assessment Centre method, AT&T's method was the quickest to gain international recognition. Their method bridged all types of cultural gaps and spread to South Africa, Australia, Great Britain and Japan as well as Germany, Scandinavia, the Philippines and even Singapore.

The growing interest in this method is due partly to the following factors:

- There is an increasing demand for a reliable method which can identify a workforce's strengths and weaknesses so that training scheme budgets can be used efficiently and effectively.
- Techniques used in selection and promotion procedures should be objective and non-discriminative.
- There is a growing awareness that not only personnel officers but also managers should be responsible for the placement of staff in their departments.
- There is a demand for assessment methods which are geared towards results.

In Western Europe the Assessment Centre is used in different countries by several organisations.

- The Netherlands: AT&T, Philips, ABN-AMRO Bank, KLM, AHOLD, ING-BANK, Mars, BSO, KPN, Shell, Sara-Lee/DE, Solvay Duphar and many others.
- Belgium: Generale Bank, BP, Ford, GM and Bekaert.
- Germany: IBM, Bayer, Ford, BAT, Agfa, BASF, Daimler Benz, CO-OP, Dunlop, Eli Lilly, Opel/GM, Pepsi.
- Italy: Montedison, Alitalia, Fiat, Amex, SIP, Pirelli, Bayer, Banco di Roma and others.

It is a method which could be easily used by small companies. It is also encouraging that an increasing number of universities are showing interest in the Assessment Centre method.

During the seventies various articles emphasised the "over-competitive side" of the Assessment Centre method. This is not in fact a very prominent aspect. Systematic evaluations of assessment programmes have been carried out and the results showed that candidates found the method challenging, fascinating, fair and educational, and hardly ever threatening, over-competitive or boring. Managers in Europe, like those in America, do not object to the group aspect of the methodology. In the first place, candidates compete against themselves rather than against each other and a little functional stress is not a bad thing.

According to various studies the following matters are considered relevant to the fair evaluation of personnel:

- The evaluation criteria should be clearly written. Candidates should be informed about them.
- The system should use a clear scale of assessment.
- The assessors should be able to observe the behaviour under assessment often.
- The assessors should be able to evaluate criteria effectively.
- More than one assessor should be used where possible.
- Candidates should have the right to make an appeal.
- Candidates should have the right to initiate an assessment (in the cases of promotion or transfer).

The Assessment Centre method complies with the first five of the above-mentioned requirements, so it is not very surprising that the Equal Employment Opportunity Commission (EEOC) has described the Assessment Centre method as being fair.

To summarise, the Assessment Centre method is both scientifically justified and practically applicable. The method is not new, it is not typically American, nor is it a passing trend, but a very useful method of bringing long-awaited changes into the personnel arena.

PART 2
The Basic Principles of the Assessment Centre

Assessment Dimensions and Situations

P.G.W. Jansen

2.1 INTRODUCTION

Initial impressions of human behaviour are that it appears to be chaotic; a tangle of widely different and rapidly-changing situations. But how can we organise this "chaos" in order to determine, for example, management potential? This can be done by attributing "dispositions", "abilities" and "traits" to the person under observation. It is assumed that these personal characteristics underly visible behaviour. Observed behaviour, in that case, is nothing more than a manifestation of these personal characteristics.

There is nothing wrong with this type of procedure, as long as it is tested, of course. However, it does have one main problem and that is that different users tend to use very different competence-, trait- or ability-rating categories and furthermore, the same dimension (verbal label) for different types of behaviour. There is no standard terminology for psychological assessment.

Assessment Centres: A Practical Handbook, P. Jansen and F. de Jongh.

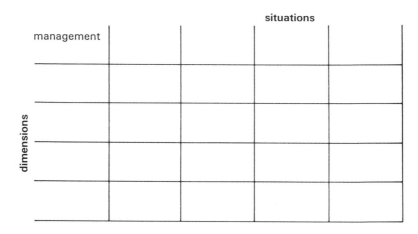

Figure 2.1   The Assessment Centre as a grid of dimensions (rating categories) and situations (situational assignments)

In this book, however, we will try to be as accurate and consistent as possible in our use of terminology.

Figure 2.1 shows the AC as a grid of assignments and assessment categories (dimensions). Dimensions appear horizontally and the AC assignments, vertically. The candidate's behaviour is written in the boxes.

Dimensions and Situations

Figure 2.2 shows how this grid can be used for an Assessment Centre for commercial management. Four assessment "dimensions" (ie the horizontal or row entries in Figure 2.1) are observed and assessed by means of four "situations" or assignments (ie the vertical classification in Figure 2.1). Not all dimensions appear in all assignments. For example, "leadership" can not be easily assessed in assignments that involve deskwork such as writing a draft for a business plan.

The term "dimension" may remind the reader of a character trait or a personal attribute. Here we will restrict ourselves to a definition based on Figure 2.1: a dimension is what the different assignments and various real work situations have in common, in terms of what they demand of the candidate. Assignments, such as giving a speech, selling, and top level negotiating, put demands on someone's verbal communication skills (see Figure 2.2). Delivering a speech, however, requires more than this. The speech has to be prepared and written in such a way that the

	situations			
dimensions	giving a speech	conducting a sales interview	top level negotiating	drafting a business plan
problem solving	0	0	+	+ +
interpersonal sensitivity	+	+ +	+ +	0
leadership	+	+ +	+ +	0
planning and organising	+	+	+ +	+ +

Figure 2.2   An example of Figure 2.1
++: very important
+: important
0: not really important

message can be clearly conveyed in a short space of time. These are situational requirements which involve other dimensions such as, problem solving, interpersonal sensitivity and planning and organising. In this way, dimensions and situations intersect, as in Figures 2.1. and 2.2.

We can conclude that Assessment Centres and real work situations can be characterised by a set of personal dispositions/ dimensions, or by a set of situational abilities/situations. The pattern of the plus and minus signs in Figure 2.2 demonstrates that not all dimensions are involved in every situation/ assignment. AC assignments can be either *heterogeneous* or *homogeneous* with respect to the number and diversity of dimensions involved.

Dimensional or Situational Assessment Centres

Chapter 1 showed that the term "Assessment Centre" is generally used to denote one part of a more elaborate selection/ promotion/development procedure, which also consists of simulations of work situations such as a simulated appraisal interview or an intelligence test. This is how we shall use the term "Assessment Centre" in this book.

In an Assessment Centre each candidate is evaluated in various situations on several criteria. Assessors observe candidates' behaviour through a "grid" consisting of personal characteristics or dimensions, and situations. An Assessment Centre should consist of at least two simulation assignments, which should stimulate distinct behaviour that is critical to the target job. During the assessors' end meeting, the assessors go through all their assessments and corresponding observations, in order to come up with one score for every dimension or situation, as well as a final score which is known as the *Overall Assessment Rating* (OAR).

"Horizontal generalisation" (across the situations) provides us with a dimensional profile of the candidate. "Vertical generalisation" (across dimensions) produces a situational profile or a skills profile. To determine the OAR, the dimensional or situational profiles are evaluated according to a predetermined criterion, ie "managerial work on the level of a senior department supervisor in the commercial sector". The OAR and corresponding dimensional or situational profiles are reported back to the candidate and/or the person in charge of the Assessment Centre, who may then use the results in personnel decisions such as recruitment rejection, training, transfer and so on.

An ability or competence refers to what someone is able to do in a specific situation, whereas a dimension or disposition indicates what someone generally *is*. A situational ability or competence denotes someone's command of a set of behavioural elements that determines effective handling of, for example, negotiating (in an AC or in real work). Therefore, an ability should always be considered in the context of effective job performance.

AC results are usually reported in the form of a dimensional profile. A dimensional AC report is made by generalising across situations. But the AC representations in Figures 2.1 and 2.2 show that a situational profile can be made from abilities. In this way, the AC report indicates how well a candidate performed in the assignments. AC's in which the performance of an assignment is evaluated and reported *within* the framework of a specific part of the job are still scarce (although their number is increasing). In view of this practice, this chapter is confined to a discussion of the most frequently used dimensions. See Chapter 5 for a treatment of AC assignments.

2.2 THE ASSESSMENT CENTRE DIMENSIONS

Every AC starts with a job analysis (see Chapter 5). According to Figure 2.1, a function can be described in two ways:

1. using dimensional terminology, such as:
   - "creativity"
   - "interpersonal sensitivity"
   - "initiative", or
2. situational terminology, which denotes the *critical* tasks that a certain job involves:
   - "conceive and interpret budget plans"
   - "managing 15 people directly and 40 indirectly"
   - "advising senior management".

It is essential that all the concepts used in dimensional and situational job descriptions transcend concrete and everyday types of behaviour. For example, "manager X scolded employee Y on 14 February 1990" should be described in terms of either a dimension: "manager X tends to act rather insensitively", or a situation: "manager X has no command of social skills in this situation".

What are the most important dimensions in Assessment Centres? In this book, we distinguish four major dimensions, the so-called *meta-dimensions*. These are:

1. powers of intelligence
2. social skills
3. powers of determination
4. will-power.

The first refers to a broad range of cognitive behaviour, the second to all kinds of communicative behaviour, the third to various forms of operational (administrative, managerial) behaviour, and the fourth to behaviour related to personal strength and tenacity (more explanations will be given shortly). Of course, the meta-dimensions themselves are far too general to be used in a practical AC. In this book they are nothing more than a framework for a more specific set of 12 AC dimensions (see Table 2.1). These dimensions should be regarded as *possible* (very feasible) AC rating categories. Another set of dimensions could be used, in which dimensions are further subdivided into *micro dimensions*, or regrouped with other meta-dimensions, in

Table 2.1 The AC (meta-) dimensions used in this book

Meta dimension	Dimension
Powers of intelligence	Problem analysis
	Problem solving
	Creativity
Social skills	Interpersonal sensitivity
	Sociability
	Leadership
Powers of determination	Planning and organizing
	Delegating and management control
Willpower	Initiative
	Persistence
	Firmness
	Decisiveness

order to make the observation and rating system more transparent. Nevertheless, on a higher, more abstract level, most sets of AC dimensions usually consist of no more than five global categories or meta-dimensions.

The Twelve Dimensions in Table 2.1

The first meta-dimension, *powers of intelligence*, not only refers to a passive kind of knowing, but also to being able to conceive new things in an active way. In other words, it is not only the power to analyse a puzzle to find the perfect solution (problem analysis), but also the power to construct new puzzles (problem analysis and creativity). The analysis should not only consist of dismantling the problem and numbering each aspect precisely, but also of synthesising the bits and pieces: a proposal, a plan, an idea, which is preferably both new (creativity) and feasible (problem solving).

The second meta-dimension, *social skills*, refers to all aspects of working with people in order to contribute to the general mission of the organisation. Interpersonal sensitivity measures a willingness to participate in a group. The candidate is not disruptive and does not whine but contributes to the larger goals of the group that he or she belongs to. The candidate does not initiate group collaboration, but follows in an open and constructive manner. Initiating behaviour is demonstrated by candidates who have the ability to direct the group towards a certain target (sociability). Using both enthusiasm and practical knowledge, this candidate determines the way in which the group is structured and the general atmosphere. He/she is inspiring. The difference between interpersonal sensitivity and sociability is that interpersonal sensitivity is passive whereas sociability is active.

The final, most developed dimension of social skills applies to a person who is able to convince other group members to follow his suggestions to enable the achievement of organisational goals with and through the group. In this case we have the most directive instance of social skills: leadership. Some individuals may possess this to such a degree that they would not bother if the group was disbanded once the goal had been achieved.

Powers of determination, the third meta-dimension, refers to someone's ability to carry out their intentions, in spite of logistic, financial or social problems. The most important aspects here are someone's operational ability to know *how*, a practical ability to plan, check and direct projects (planning and organising), and efficient management of an agenda. A second aspect of powers of determination is control via delegation and management of marginal conditions (delegating and management control). In this book we use two general dimensions of powers of determination. The first, planning and organising, is crucial to every type of function; and the second, delegating and management control, is essential for management functions in particular.

The fourth meta-dimension, *willpower*, consists of four dimensions. First, a candidate has to start "all on his own" (initiative), instead of waiting passively for some form of instruction. When the candidate is engaged in action, he should not give up lightly, but proceed using his initiative (persistence). If the candidate is put under pressure, he should hold his own (firmness), even if he is put in a situation that is very difficult to change or influence. The difference between persistence and firmness is that in the first case, it is the candidate who exerts the pressure, whereas in the second case the stress stems from an external source and more or less "happens to" the candidate. This distinction may seem rather subtle, but psychologically there is a difference between self-inflicted stress and external stress which is inflicted on someone and cannot be manipulated. The first type of stress can be coped with and may even be nice; "pep-stress", for instance. External pressures (firmness) may not be so pleasant. The end product of these three stages and corresponding dimensions of willpower is someone's capacity to determine their own policies, to "be in control", and to make, in a self-assured and assertive way, independent and deliberated choices (decisiveness). The candidate dares to take a point of view and calculated risks.

2.3   TYPES OF DIMENSIONS

Primary and Secondary Dimensions

The list that was shown in the previous section should not be regarded as a definitive classification of AC dimensions. The type of dimensions is dependent on the specific aims of an AC and the actual assignments. Table 2.1 can be used to select AC dimensions. One should start with the meta-dimensions (ACs usually include all four meta-dimensions) and then go on to choose a set of specific dimensions. If this is done in reverse, ie starting with a long list of possible dimensions, it tends to get bogged down in lengthy discussions about terminology. It is best to adopt terms that are familiar to the organisation in question. If one knows what dimensions are required at meta-level, one should formulate these by referring to the following considerations:

Do the dimensions:
- relect what the AC contractor wants to measure?
- conform with the type of terminology and language that is used by the contracting organisation?
- fit in with the candidates (the feedback that they receive will use terminology that is based on this set of dimensions)?
- consist of phrasings that do not overlap and are not interchangeable?

It is important to avoid so-called "container concepts"; terms that encompass a very broad range of behaviour. As a rule, a term that refers to more than one dimension cannot be used in an AC. Flexibility, for example, is a popular AC dimension. However, it should not be considered as a primary personal dimension, since it cannot be interpreted or assessed without some sort of contextual reference. For example: are we dealing with flexibility in terms of someone's powers of intelligence or social skills? In the first case, flexibility coincides with creativity. In the second case, contextual information is needed. In the context of interpersonal sensitivity, flexibility simply coincides with social adaptability. In the context of leadership, however, it refers to a broad range of socially influential abilities. Finally, flexibility in the context of powers of determination generally refers to someone's ability to improvise or organise.

In the same way, a dimension such as powers of negotiation can be defined as: "making and maintaining effective contacts, directed at achieving a consensus of opinion as well as maintaining one's own standpoint, but giving in where necessary" and is much easier to assess when it is conceived as a composite of several primary dimensions. From the above definition we can identify the following personal characteristics: sociability ("making and maintaining contacts"), leadership ("effective"), planning and organising ("directed at . . ."), persistence ("keeping to one's own standpoints") and decisiveness ("giving in where necessary"). In this way, negotiating should not be considered as a single AC dimension, but as a cocktail of dimensions and according to the conception of an AC depicted in Table 2.1, as a situation, that is *a specific task*. This is why negotiating was used as an example of a critical situation in Figure 2.2.

Missing Dimensions

The assessment category *motivation* has not been included in the list of dimensions in Table 2.1. Contrary to willpower, motivation refers to the specific reasons that "drive" a candidate in his or her (working) life. Motivation can be assessed by identifying the candidate's driving force; what makes him or her "tick". Motivation is, of course, an important determinant of working behaviour, but an AC is not really designed to find out what motivates candidates – the candidate himself may not even know. Determining a candidate's motivation would require far deeper probing, and interaction between an assessor and a candidate in which the assessor should adopt an active approach. The best method for assessing a candidate's motivation is an interview specifically designed for this purpose. A lot of training and experience is required to conduct this type of interview effectively. This is why motivation interviews are often conducted by psychologists.

In the same way, ACs are not designed to assess intelligence. An intelligence test is, of course, a type of situational exercise, since it stimulates candidates to demonstrate all kinds of intelligent behaviour, on the spot, which is then carefully recorded and evaluated. There is, however, one important difference between the intelligence test and an AC. ACs use assignments (or "items") that involve behaviour that is specific to real work, whereas intelligence tests do not. Viewed from the perspective of "real work", an intelligence test consists of rather peculiar and sometimes even "eccentric" assignments like, for example, the mental rotation of figures, or filling in verbal analogies.

Another assessment category that is not included in Table 2.1 is professional knowledge pertaining to specific kinds of business understanding, or organisational knowledge (being able to read a balance-sheet, for example). This does not mean that concrete knowledge and understanding of logistics, commerce or finance will *not* be required in an assignment. Often assignments that involve organisational knowledge do not aim at testing the level of someone's knowledge, but whether he/she is able to *apply* that knowledge in the context of an actual organisation.

2.4   RECENT DEVELOPMENTS

Initially, the term "Assessment Centre" referred to a set of simulations of real work. However, this "core" is frequently combined with other assessment instruments, such as intelligence tests, personality questionnaires and interviews. Since the term "Assessment Centre" is not protected by copyright, every assessment procedure can be called by that name. This is exactly what is happening at the moment. Nevertheless, there are three main trends in the use of AC assessment dimensions:

1. There is a growing tendency for dimensions to be derived from the contracting organisation. They are no longer "superimposed" by an external agency, but developed in the corporation itself. In the process of developing and constructing an AC that corresponds to existing human resource management practices, the organisation is made aware of what comprises relevant assessment categories. This process of discovering and formulating implicit appraisal criteria is, in itself, extremely constructive to the organisation, apart from the other benefits that the actual AC will bring. This process

makes management aware of the type of criteria on which personnel are evaluated, and also confronts them with the question of whether they require employees with this type of profile.

   An additional advantage is that the final AC profile is not only management "property", but is also formulated in the type of language that management is used to. For example, in some organisations "helicopter view" has a clear and precise meaning, but in others the same term is meaningless; they may use instead terms such as "thinking power" or "vision" to denote the same thing.

2. Some people want to abandon the use of dimensions in ACs altogether. In this case, assessors no longer discuss their individual dimensional ratings with one another in order to resolve large score differences. Instead, the various dimensional ratings serve as a starting point for a discussion about the meaning and interpretation of the observed (situational) behaviour of each candidate. In this way, dimensions are only used to classify and label behaviour and not as vehicles for discussion. Assessors talk about what they saw (observed behaviour), and how they evaluate what they saw, in their own way.

3. There is a tendency to reduce the number of dimensions used in ACs. This is, of course, closely related to the second development. Beforehand, assessors had to become acquainted with the precise meaning of 10 to 15 dimensions, the set of assessment categories is now limited to between five and seven dimensions. Sometimes these are even formulated on a type of meta-level.

Chapter 3

Assessment Centre Assignments

P.G.W. Jansen

3.1 INTRODUCTION

A standard repertoire of Assessment Centre assignments has evolved over the years. An AC designed to evaluate management potential, for example, will always include simulations of managers coming into contact with employees – a simulation of an evaluation interview, and paperwork – the renowned "In-basket" assignment, which requires candidates to deal with the contents of a typical manager's in-tray. In this chapter we will discuss the most frequently used assignments. We will examine which assignments are most effective in testing specific dimensions and/or skills (see Chapter 2 for a description of dimensions and skills). The predictive value of the Assessment Centre will be dealt with in Chapter 14.

Table 3.1 indicates the most common AC assignments. They are divided into two groups. Firstly, simulations that have been used so often that they have begun to lead a life of their own.

Assessment Centres: A Practical Handbook, P. Jansen and F. de Jongh.
© 1997 John Wiley & Sons Ltd.

Table 3.1 Assessment Centre assignments and relevant dimensions

Dimensions	Assignments							
	1	2	3	4	5	6	7	8
Problem analysis	X	X	X	X	X	X	X	
Problem solving	X	X	X	X	X	X	X	
Creativity	X	X	X	X			X	X
Interpersonal sensitivity	X	X		X	X	X		X
Sociability		X		X	X	X		
Leadership		X	X	X	X	X		
Delegating/management control	X				X		X	
Planning/organising	X	X	X				X	
Initiative	X	X	X	X		X		
Persistence		X	X	X	X	X		
Firmness		X	X	X				
Decisiveness	X	X	X	X	X	X		X
	1	2	3	4	5	6	7	8

1 = In-basket
2 = Group discussion
3 = Fact-finding
4 = Presentation
5 = Dialogue
6 = Meeting
7 = Planning
8 = Memorandum

They consist of the In-basket, the Group Discussion, the Fact-finding assignment, the Presentation and the Dialogue. They are no longer regarded as simulations of actual work situations, but as Assessment Centre tests.

The other tests can be regarded as the everyday tasks that are involved in real work. They are more or less exact copies of work situations and are restricted to a certain place and time. These assignments can be designed to imitate the type of problems and critical situations that one might encounter in the target job. They come in many different varieties.

Table 3.1 indicates which assignments are most important for which dimensions. This is a rather liberal interpretation. In principle, each assignment can elicit every type of behaviour.

It is also possible to ignore the dimension scores and evaluate the overall performance of an assignment. The guidelines for such an evaluation consist of questions like:

- Did the candidate tackle the problem well, on the whole?
- Did the candidate deal with the problem effectively?
- Was his/her approach adequate?

Then a final evaluation can be made of the candidate's performance.

Table 3.1 can be seen as the "first cause" of all Assessment Centres. After all, an AC is nothing more than a selection of assignments (between 3 and 5) and dimensions (5 and 10). We shall focus upon the most important assignments, using the order in which they are listed in Table 3.1.

3.2 ASSIGNMENTS

In-basket

The In-basket is a simulation of an employee's in-tray. The In-basket contains a wide variety of hand-written and typed documents: telephone messages, scribbled notes, memos, policy documents, letters of complaint, orders, personnel information (for example a letter of application or a promotion recommendation). These are referred to as items. The candidate is given an in-tray, which includes between 10 and 25 items. Sometimes the documents are well-addressed, sometimes they are meant for someone else. It is not always clear what type of response is expected. The In-basket instructions are usually phrased as follows:

'You have . . . hours for the In-basket assignment (including the reading of instructions). You should do this in the role of . . . (fictitious name) who works for . . . (fictitious company, government institution etc). You have been employed by this company for . . . months and are reasonably settled in. Today is . . . day . . . 19 . . . On your desk you will find a rather full in-tray. It contains a number of letters, memos and so forth. You have . . . hours in which to deal with these various items. The items are quite varied, some are more important than others. Due to a very busy period a backlog has built up. You have reserved . . . hours to deal with this.
It is your task to undertake suitable action for each in-tray item, as if you were carrying out this task in real life. You should state your reaction to each item and your reasons for this. In real life, you would probably deal with some of these items by phone. In this assignment, however, all your reactions should be written. However, if you do decide that an item would be better dealt with by phone, you should write down who you would contact and what you wish to discuss, when and with what aim.
You are assessed on your written reactions. You will not be able to explain your actions once the assignment has been completed, therefore it is important to make a (short) note of your considerations and make sure that your reactions to the various items are written as clearly and comprehensively as possible, and state the reasons why you chose a specific line of action. If you wish to make an appointment with someone, write down what you wish to discuss, when and with whom, as

well as what you wish to achieve with this discussion. Even if you decide
to postpone action to a later date, you should still follow these guidelines
– stating which line of action you would take, why, when and who this
would involve.'

The candidate is usually given two to three hours to deal with
the in-tray. In some Assessment Centres he/she is also expected
to carry out some of the suggested lines of action, for example
write a draft for a letter in reply to a complaint. But it is usually
sufficient to state exactly what one should do and why.

Often the In-basket instruction is accompanied by several
pages of background information on the fictitious organisation.
These include organisation schemes, a (rather incomplete)
agenda, and a short description of the history of the company.
Sometimes short descriptions of employees are provided. The
candidate is not expected to react to this background information, but use it for reference purposes during the assignment.
Candidates are very clearly told that they are only assessed on
what they write down. This forces candidates to make their
reactions as clear and comprehensive as possible.

Sometimes the actual In-basket is preceded by an example of
an In-basket item. This gives the candidate some idea of what is
expected. A model item is shown in Figure 3.1 and a model
answer is shown in Figure 3.2.

The In-basket is a typical simulation of desk work. It puts high
demands on skills like organising, structuring, planning (problem analysis), as well as finding an adequate approach (problem
solving and creativity). It is important to maintain an overview
of the sometimes concrete, sometimes irritatingly vague and ap-
parently isolated problems included in the separate items. In
this way one can form an idea of the organisation's problems as
a whole. The In-basket assignment puts specific demands on
one's powers of intelligence.

In the In-basket assignment, someone's social skills can only
be measured on paper. We gain some idea of the candidate's
social intelligence, social insight (interpersonal sensitivity), but
little or no insight into social aptitude (sociability, leadership).
Someone may respond to a certain In-basket item by saying that
he/she will have "a good talk" with an employee, but this does
not mean to say that he/she is able to do this in practice.

As a rule, In-basket behaviour is evaluated on categories like
planning and organising, delegation and management control,
interpersonal sensitivity, problem analysis, problem solving and

from: William Fairfax
to: John Smith
subject: arriving late
date: 7 October 1987

When we first met you said that I could always come to you with
any problems. I would like to ask your advice about the following.
Carter, who does a lot of the administrative work in my group, is
always late for work. As you know, we do have flexi-time, but we
are expected to begin between 7.30 and 9.00 a.m. Carter, however,
always arrives around 9.15. If I approach him on this, he always
replies by saying that he works hard and that his work is always
ready on time, which is true. But I don't think that it would be fair
to the other colleagues if I made an exception for Carter. Could I
discuss this with you?

William Fairfax

Figure 3.1 Example of an In-basket item included in the instructions

decisiveness. But the answers can be so varied that the In-basket
also includes assessment on motivational dimensions, ie
willpower.

Group Discussion

Some candidates are asked to solve a problem with a group of
other candidates and are assigned an hour to do so. The candidates are given the chance to look at the problem beforehand.
The best size for a group is about six candidates. Assessors
(there are often as many assessors as candidates) are present
during the meeting. They observe and take notes. No one

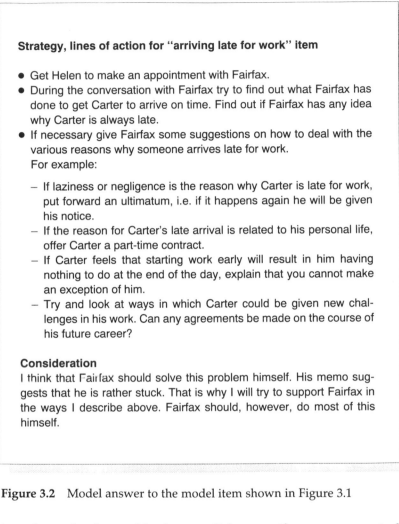

Strategy, lines of action for "arriving late for work" item

- Get Helen to make an appointment with Fairfax.
- During the conversation with Fairfax try to find out what Fairfax has done to get Carter to arrive on time. Find out if Fairfax has any idea why Carter is always late.
- If necessary give Fairfax some suggestions on how to deal with the various reasons why someone arrives late for work.
  For example:

  - If laziness or negligence is the reason why Carter is late for work, put forward an ultimatum, i.e. if it happens again he will be given his notice.
  - If the reason for Carter's late arrival is related to his personal life, offer Carter a part-time contract.
  - If Carter feels that starting work early will result in him having nothing to do at the end of the day, explain that you cannot make an exception of him.
  - Try and look at ways in which Carter could be given new challenges in his work. Can any agreements be made on the course of his future career?

Consideration

I think that Fairfax should solve this problem himself. His memo suggests that he is rather stuck. That is why I will try to support Fairfax in the ways I describe above. Fairfax should, however, do most of this himself.

Figure 3.2 Model answer to the model item shown in Figure 3.1

interferes further with the candidates – they are expected to solve the problem themselves.

The group has to decide how it will do this: will they elect a person to chair the discussion, or a secretary who makes notes of the decision or keeps an eye on the time? The way in which the discussion is conducted and its contents are left open. The assignment however is not open. On the contrary, the group are often presented with urgent problems, and put under a lot of pressure. They may have to address problems like the need for quick and drastic cutbacks; redundancies (which employees should be made redundant?); the rearrangement of rooms (great differences in size or lack of space); crucial investments; or how to allocate a small budget.

In order to start a discussion, this assignment is designed as a mixture between cooperation (arriving at a decision together) and competition (looking after one's own interests). Furthermore, the candidates are allowed to study the issues beforehand so that they can get straight down to business during the actual discussion. In this way candidates do not waste time with explanations. After roughly 45 minutes, the Group Discussion is brought to an end by the director of the AC (see Chapter 8). The assessors then make their assessment. In most cases each manager makes an assessment of each candidate. Compared to the In-basket, the Group Discussion has a greater focus on the breadth of someone's argument. Social skills, decisivenes and willpower are also important.

Fact Finding

Once more a candidate is presented with a problem. This time he/she does not have to come up with a solution, but sensible questions. Afterwards, these questions will be presented to the role-player, while the assessors watch and listen. In the analysis phase, the candidate has to not only find out what the case involves, but what it does *not* involve, ie which essential information is missing. This demands another approach; the candidate has to formulate questions in a creative and investigative way so that more information is revealed about the issue at stake. After the question and answer game with the role-player, the candidate is given a short space of time in which to make a decision and put forward a solution. Often this is followed by a short discussion, during which the role-player challenges the candidate's line of argument.

Obviously, the Fact-finding assignment puts high demands on someone's powers of intelligence in terms of breadth and depth: creativity, knowledge of "business approaches" such as logistics, finances, personnel and organisation, commerce and so on. When gathering the missing information, the candidate should be as thorough as possible (first in breadth then in depth). The candidate should be on the lookout for missing pieces of information and aware of the implications of certain pieces of information. The second measurement of dimensional assessment is decisiveness: the candidate has to bring something about. Social skills are also important, in terms of lending an attentive ear to the contact person, and asking him/her the right questions.

Presentation

As in the case of the Group discussion and the Fact-finding assignment, the candidate is given half an hour to prepare for the delivery. This is carried out in front of assessors. Once more a fictitious problem is involved. Now the emphasis is on trying to find out what is going on. At first the material which is presented for analysis appears rather disorganised, chaotic even. The candidate has to form an idea of the problem at hand based on this material, and then present this idea to a delegation from the same company (assessors). Once the candidate has related as much of the information as possible without interruption, stated what he/she thinks is wrong and put forward a solution, the assessors are allowed to ask questions.

This assignment puts specific demands on someone's powers of intelligence, social skills and willpower. In this way, it is quite similar to Fact Finding, but with more emphasis on making a plan, putting forward suggestions (synthetic ability) that are realistic enough to be carried out. Moreover, the candidate's behaviour is crucial. He/she should be able to hold his/her own, relate the facts and expose the truth in a nice way and so on. The cross pattern Table 3.1 does not indicate as much, but compared to the Fact-finding assignment, the Presentation demands far more of the candidate in terms of social skills and willpower. Otherwise, the Presentation tests the same skills as in the previous assignments: planning, setting a target, investigating, taking part in a meeting, negotiating.

Dialogue

Most ACs include a Dialogue with a role-player, which deals with a different situation according to the aims of each AC. It may, for example, simulate a sales conversation, in which the role-player is a client and the candidate the salesperson, or an evaluation interview, between a manager and an employee of a production company. The candidate would be given a concise description of the far from optimal work progress of one of the production groups that falls under his/her control. The candidate is then given some time to prepare for the interview with the group manager (role-player). In this conversation, the candidate should achieve a number of targets that have been set beforehand. This assignment is observed by two trained assessors and the candidate is given scores on certain dimensions, in this case management behaviour.

This is, however, one example of an endless number of variations. The actual contents of the assignment determine the type of demands that are put on the candidate's intelligence. Even so the role-player's script determines to what extent the social skills or willpower should be tested. The situational determination of this type of test, and situational tests in general, is very high. This is why we have been so liberal in our placing of crosses in Table 3.1.

Other Assignments

Examples of situational tests that are less frequently used are the simulation of a meeting involving more than one role-player, the planning assignment (for example involving a logistic problem, i.e. the removal of head office) or writing a piece (e.g. about an important social issue). The first example involves imitation of actual social behaviour whereas the other two involve management desk-work. In effect, the last two could be seen as separate items of an In-basket.

In contrast to the five classic assignments, the titles of the other three indicate clearly what the assignments involve. They are always simulations of the familiar types of tasks that usually take up a half to one hour of an actual work day. Everyone takes part in meeting once in a while or plans and writes a memo.

The skills that are tested in these assignments are often the same as the assignment itself. The best example of this is the planning assignment, which tests someone's planning ability within a certain organisational context. The assessment of planning is as broad as the assignment is inclusive. As the range of the assignment becomes broader, ie involves more varied types of behaviour, the necessity (and certainly the tendency) to assess on a larger number of skills or else dimensions will increase (see Chapter 7).

3.3 CANDIDATE PREPARATION

Assessment Centres work best when candidates are well informed about what they should expect. From an ethical point of view, it is only right that candidates should know what to expect. A tactical line of approach is underhand. There are organisations that "drop" candidates in Assessment Centres with little or no preparation, in the belief that one can only see what someone is worth by throwing them into the deep end. This is questionable. The AC claims to observe people as they really are and not how they behave in exceptional situations caused by panic and nervousness. The Assessment Centre is geared towards eliciting and assessing behaviour, because this gives a visible indication of what a person is worth and is a good predictor of future behaviour. The actual AC is preceded by instructions designed to remove any obstacles that prevent candidates from showing their real behaviour – an important factor. Irrelevant behaviour is determined by the aim of the AC. As a rule there are two possible aims: the AC is used to assess either the performance of candidates on a number of critical aspects of the job, or the candidate's future potential. In the last case, the actual performance is not what counts but the way (speed, thoroughness, breadth, depth) in which the candidate learns new skills (that are needed, for example, for sorting through, organising and dealing with the items in an in-tray in the In-basket assignment). The Assessment Centre measures what someone can do or what someone is capable of doing in the near future.

During the AC it is the performance of the assignments that counts, which is why it is so crucial to exclude disruptive influences like unfamiliarity with the AC's methods, for example. In order to ensure that an accurate assessment has been made of an assignment, it may be necessary for candidates to perform certain assignments twice. In this case the second attempt would be used in the evaluation; The first attempt is more of a practice run. In the In-basket assignment, for example, the same effect could also be achieved by practising one item, before carrying out the actual assignment – see Figure 3.1 – and focusing on which elements should be included in the right answer.

Research has proven that there is a marked improvement in the second attempt compared with the first one. The effect of this practice run is easily discerned. With the second In-basket, differences between candidates are indicative of what they are really worth. From this point irrelevant behaviour, for example, reading into the assignment to get an idea of the best way to tackle a complicated assignment like the In-basket, becomes

Table 3.2 Measurement of performance or potential by means of two In-basket assignments (or one In-basket preceded by a practice item)

Basis for assessment	Measurement	
	Biased	Unbiased
Performance	1st In-basket	2nd In-basket (or 1st + practice item)
Potential	2nd In-basket	Difference between 1st and 2nd In-basket

totally unimportant. In this case, the first In-basket or In-basket item serves as a step towards real In-basket behaviour.

But if the AC is geared towards assessing potential, the difference between the first and the second In-basket is interesting. If the difference is small, this shows that the candidate is good at adapting to new situations and work. If the difference is great, then it shows that the candidate needs more time to get used to new material. So if the AC is concerned with how quickly people get used to working with new material, then the difference between the first and the second In-basket is interesting. But if the onus is upon assessing how well someone manipulates simulated job behaviour, then it is only the second In-basket that counts (see Table 3.2 for an overview).

3.4 CONCLUSION

In this chapter we have dealt with the most prominent Assessment Centre assignments. It is important to stress that an Assessment Centre would not exist without assignments. A lot of renewal has taken place in this area (and far less in the dimension area). Making specific assignments (see "Other assignments") is not as difficult as it may seem, as long as the Assessment Centre constructor is well informed of the type of behaviour that the AC should measure, and the person who is currently employed in the job on which the AC is based, can supply descriptions of relevant critical situations. These can then be noted down and rewritten according to the AC; the level of the candidate and the dimensions on which the AC is based.

Chapter 4

Managers as Assessors

M.J.C. de Graaff

4.1 INTRODUCTION

The success of the use of ACs within organisations is highly dependent upon the careful selection and training of assessors. Research carried out by General Motors (GM) in 1988, revealed that the number of hours dedicated to training corresponded with the quality of predictions made by assessors. Two groups of GM managers were trained as assessors. One group followed a two-day training programme, whilst the other followed a four-day training programme. The latter group were able to make far more accurate and valid judgements than the former.

Until now, most of the organisations that used the AC method opted for internal assessors from their own managerial staff. The selection and training of internal assessors should be carried out thoroughly. These subjects are pursued in greater detail in the following sections (4.2 and 4.3). Often it is difficult for organisations to decide who they should choose for the job. More attention is given to this in section 4.4.

Assessment Centres: A Practical Handbook, P. Jansen and F. de Jongh.
© 1997 John Wiley & Sons Ltd.

4.2   SELECTING MANAGER-ASSESSORS

A list of standard criteria for the selection of potential assessors does not exist. The following considerations, however, have always played an essential role in the choice of managers:

- First, one should find out which level the potential assessor should occupy within the organisation's hierarchy. This is dependent upon the aims of the AC. If, for example, the aim of the AC is to select top management potential, then top management should be approached and made aware of the crucial role that assessors play within an organisation. Assessors determine who will be responsible for an organisation's future activities and development. Generally it can be assumed that the higher the assessor's position, the greater the AC's effectiveness as an instrument of selection and assessment.
- It is also important to find out which managers are really interested, and actually involved, in personnel management. When the AC method is first used in an organisation, it is a good idea to have a few assessors who openly support AC technology. They play a crucial role in arousing enthusiasm for the AC method and eventually ensuring its acceptance. Again, the higher in the company these assessors are placed, the better.
- If a company's use of ACs is sporadic there would be no point in using internal assessors, instead it would be better to contract an AC (see section 4.4). Assessors should be actively involved in an AC at least three times a year, otherwise they will not be able to gain enough in-depth knowledge.
- To guarantee accurate assessments, assessors should start by observing one candidate at a time (see section 4.3). For AC sessions involving group discussions between four and six candidates, for example, a minimum of four to six assessors would have to be trained. This amount can be reduced if the group consists of three role-players and three candidates. In this case three assessors could be used. This method would, however, be costly, since as well as the assessors and role-players, a director would need to be employed (an advisor who supervises assessors, see Chapter 8), and the logistics of the operation would be complicated. When assessors have acquired enough experience of registering behaviour, they

can go on to observing more than one candidate at a time, in group simulations, for example.

Apart from these considerations, the most important link in the selection process is the person responsible for choosing the assessors, who is known as a selector. The selector is usually a P&O director or head of the personnel department. The selector has to determine who could be and would like to be an assessor. If the selector approaches the "wrong" managers, the AC may never get off the ground. It only takes a few "No's" to deter others from taking part.

Finally we can conclude that the criterion "suitability", does not play a major role in the selection of assessors. Any manager can learn assessor skills, although some will learn more quickly than others. Motivation is one of the most important criteria for determining which managers a selector should approach.

Readiness to participate involves the following:

- Finding time to act as an AC assessor at least three times a year, and in the first year following an assessor training course which consists of several days.
- Being prepared to discuss personal preferences and prejudices regarding an employee.
- Being open in evaluation discussions, being prepared to accept criticism and if necessary, adjust scores accordingly.

The selection of a cooperative and effectively functioning team of assessors is not an easy task. The selector has to review each manager separately. The manager should be willing to act as an assessor. The following criteria also play a role in the selection process.

- (hierarchical) position
- seniority with regards to age and experience
- the relationship between the various potential assessors.

4.3 TRAINING MANAGER-ASSESSORS

Once a group of assessors has been selected, assessor training takes place. This should be carried out one to four weeks before the start of the AC. If the time lapse is longer than five weeks, assessors may forget important aspects of their training. It is best to plan assessor training courses as near to the AC as possible.

The contents of the assessor training programme are dependent upon the contents of the AC. Each assessor training course should deal with the following subjects:

1. Introduction to the Assessment Centre Method (ACM)
2. Job analysis
3. AC dimensions
4. Assessor skills
5. Practical assignments in the AC
6. Dimensions in practical assignments
7. Role-play techniques
8. Organisation and implementation of an AC.

Introduction to the AC Method

This consists of a general introduction to the background, history, philosophy and ethical standards of the Assessment Centre Method. The ethical standards state the way in which an AC should be carried out and according to which conditions. The ethical standards also stipulate the standard requirements for assessors, the number of assessors required per candidate and the standard requirements of the final report.

Job Analysis

A job analysis is carried out so that managers can understand how a job can be translated into dimensions (see Chapter 5). The "critical incident" plays a crucial role in this understanding. A critical incident is a moment in a certain job during which the employee is not allowed to make one single mistake, since the risk of causing considerable damage is high. Some examples of critical incidents are:

- selecting personnel;
- evaluating credit applications which involve large amounts of money (banking);
- accidents, disasters, robberies (transport branch, retail, heavy industry, banks);
- taking-off and landing (pilot).

Generally it can be assumed that every job has a maximum number of critical incidents. In a commercial job, for example, dealing with clients should not be regarded as a critical incident, because that would mean that the job constantly involved critical situations. Dealing with an angry customer or a customer's complaints, however, could be regarded as a critical incident, and in this case perfect performance is necessary. The type of behaviour (translated into dimensions) required in critical incidents should be seen as crucial to successful job performance (see Chapter 5).

AC Dimensions

This involves an in-depth treatment of the dimensions which the manager-assessors should be able to recognise and evaluate during the actual AC. This usually entails becoming acquainted with and investigating (in terms of behaviour and examples of behaviour) about ten dimensions. During a later stage of training, examples of behaviour are matched with practical assignments, so that manager-assessors can recognise how and when certain behaviour is stimulated (by a role-player) and how it can be observed.

Assessor Skills

This involves studying and practising the following assessor skills:

- *Observation*: noting all the candidate does and says in relation to the role-player or to the other candidates' behaviour.
- *Registration*: making notes of everything a candidate says and does.
- *Classification*: relating the various types of behaviour to the relevant dimensions.
- *Quantifying*: giving each dimension a score.
- *Evaluation*: reaching a final score based on the scores per dimension.
- *Reporting*: to the candidate and, with the candidate's consent, to the organisation who contracted the AC.

Managers tend to have great difficulty observing and registering behaviour. Like most people they tend to base conclusions about behaviour on their own interpretations instead of on concrete evidence.

Example: If a candidate is leaning back in his chair and a trainee-assessor is asked to assess his behaviour, this often prompts answers like "he is lazy, disinterested", etc. An accurate description of a candidate's behaviour in this case would be, "He is leaning back in his chair."

Following on from this, manager-assessors find it difficult to make detailed notes on a candidate's behaviour during practical assignments. They should be reminded constantly that their notes are the only sources of classification. Classification is impossible without notes. Since each assessor has to observe and register the behaviour of more than one candidate, it would be impossible for an assessor to reproduce what a candidate said or did, without being able to refer to notes. Without notes only global indications can be made of a candidate. Registering or making notes entails nothing more than writing down what a candidate did or said during a certain assignment. This behaviour is written in the same way as a script. A certain level of self-discipline is required to register everything, and in this case, as in most others, practice makes perfect! During each assessor training, it is guaranteed that the deepest sighs of relief are heard when the first registration assignment is over. This consists of a 20 minute-long video. During actual ACs assessors take far longer than this.

The most difficult assessor skill is classifying; coupling types of behaviour to the various dimensions under assessment. Basing their conclusions upon the observed behaviour, the manager-assessor is expected to determine which behaviour should be linked with which dimension. Effective classification is something that improves with practice. Experienced assessors are quick to recognise which types of behaviour belong to which dimension. Since only a limited number of dimensions (those essential for successful job performance) are evaluated in an AC, this means that not all the behaviour that has been registered can be related to the dimensions under assessment. The rest of the registered behaviour could be listed under other, less important dimensions, but this would be rather pointless since the final assessment does not take any other dimensions into account.

During training, assessors are given a lot of time to practice classification. The essence of classification is being able to recognise behaviour and relate it to the dimensions under assessment. If this is not given enough attention, assessors will only be able to assess behaviour in a global way. They will end up giving scores without being able to support their choice with clear examples. When these types of assessors reach the final evaluation discussions and are asked to support their assessments, they give either the wrong examples or put forward very vague and general examples. This would result in their scores being excluded from the final analysis.

The prerequisite of effective assessment is accurate evaluation of behaviour. Deviations from this standard inevitably lead to generalisations and interpretative methods of assessment.

Quantifying means considering all the classified examples of behaviour and giving each candidate a score per dimension. This is the most subjective part of the entire AC process. When can we speak of "sufficient initiative", for example? Assessors will probably hold different opinions on this and award different scores as a consequence. Internal assessors should try to standardise their scores. Standardisation takes place during evaluation discussions (see below).

The assessor skill "evaluating" takes place during evaluation discussions with other assessors. During this, assessors compare the various scores (per candidate) and investigate any differences. Each assessor should be able to support his score with examples of behaviour and put his findings open to discussion. Simulated evaluation discussions take place during training, so that assessors can practice this skill.

The final skill to be dealt with is "reporting". Each assessor should be able to write an assessment report and provide candidates with feedback on their performance during the AC. These tasks are usually performed by an (internal) AC advisor, who is in some cases accompanied by an assessor. See Chapter 10 on reporting.

Practical Assignments

The implementation of practical assignments in the Assessment Centre (see also Chapter 3). It is essential that all assessors have personal experience of how each assignment is constructed and how it works. The best way to achieve this is to have a turn at being a candidate during training.

Dimensions in Practical Assignments

This involves studying the specific moments during practical assignments when dimension-related behaviour can be well observed or stimulated by a role-player. If this is given enough attention, classification becomes a lot easier, since assessors learn to recognise when and during which assignments specific dimensions can be observed. This in turn gives them more room to observe corresponding behaviour during practical assignments.

Role-play Techniques

The role-player is used to stimulate candidates to act in a certain way.

Example: A situational assignment involving a dialogue between a role-player and a candidate. If the role-player says "I have worked hard for years", he is, in effect, inviting the candidate to express sensitive behaviour. If the candidate replies "Yes, you are right. I really respect you for that", then his response is evaluated as positive sensitivity behaviour. If the candidate ignores the role-player or replies "Yes, and you are well paid for it", his response is seen as negative sensitivity behaviour. The situation demands sensitivity. If the candidate responds by paying a compliment, this will be given a positive score. If the candidate does not respond sensitively, this is given a negative score. In both cases the candidate is evaluated on the dimension "interpersonal sensitivity." This example shows how difficult classification is. Not only does demonstrated behaviour need to be classified (coupled with the relevant dimensions) but also behaviour that was desired but not demonstrated during the reconstruction. See Chapter 6 for role-players' behaviour.

Organisation and Implementation of an AC

It is important for managers to have some insight into how an AC should be organised and implemented, ie the contents of an AC and its practical and logistic organisation, as well as the use of ACs as an instrument of personnel management. Depending on the number of practical assignments that are used during the actual AC, the training course will last several days. If less time is used, the quality of the assessments will suffer. Being able to classify effectively on the basis of registered behaviour is something which demands a certain amount of training.

Final Remarks

Although it is not common practice, more and more people tend to feel that manager-assessors should be formally evaluated on their suitability. In this case, an external advisor/trainer should be asked to comment upon the assessor skills of each manager. Suitability could be based partly on performance during training and partly on assessment work during the first AC. In the last case, it would be advisable to employ the assessor under evaluation as a shadow assessor. An experienced assessor would carry out the actual assessment work, allowing the shadow assessor to observe, make notes, classify and so forth, so that the assessor's skills could be well observed and evaluated. Authorisation would depend on this performance. If an assessor failed the test extra training should be followed. This involves extra expenses, of course, but the need for well-trained assessors should not be underestimated. After all, the results of an AC can determine the course of someone's career.

4.4   THE PROS AND CONS OF WORKING WITH MANAGER-ASSESSORS

Practical experience over the past ten years has revealed a number of pros and cons in working with manager-assessors. Firstly, it is expensive. There is a lot of time and money involved in manager-assessors (see Chapter 14). As was previously mentionedj in section 4.2, assessors should realise that they have to invest a great deal of time in the first year. They have to follow assessor training courses and participate in at least three ACs per year. Direct and indirect costs of assessor training courses can be considerable. But in the long term these costs will be more than compensated for, when selection, promotion and management development (see Chapter 15) decisions turn out to be valid and well founded. The number of mistakes in placements will also be drastically reduced.

If an organisation expects to use ACs often, it is far cheaper to use internal assessors than hiring a specialised assessment bureau.

The quality of assessors is put at risk if they are not given sufficient training. Formal evaluations of their suitability almost entirely excludes the risk of low quality assessors. Economising on training time inevitably results in inadequate implementation of the AC and inaccurate personnel decisions.

The most important advantages of working with assessor-managers are:

- If (top) managers act as assessors (see section 4.2), management support is guaranteed. If the AC is conducted without manager-assessors, it is more difficult to get management support.
- Working with manager-assessors forces (top) managers to be actively involved with the development and progress of their work force. In this way responsibility for management development or promotional decisions is very definitely in the hands of line management. As assessors they are constantly concerned with the (future) suitability of employees.
- Assessor training strengthens managers' people-management skills. They learn how to assess concrete behaviour, which enables them to observe and assess employees effectively, and provide guidance.
- Manager-assessors know their organisation inside out and are more able to give the "right" score to candidate dimensions than external assessment specialists. The standardisation of scores conforms with what an organisation understands as "normal". External assessors do not have as much insight into the appropriate degree of standardisation, and must conduct research into a company before attempting to evaluate candidates.

Chapter 5

Developing an Assessment Centre

P. van Leest

5.1 INTRODUCTION

Assessment Centres (ACs) are measuring instruments. They measure the behaviour of a participant in a structured way, enabling assessors to predict the participant's future behaviour. Their development should include the following elements. First, one should determine what type of behaviour is crucial to the job in question, and then make sure that this type of behaviour can occur as much as possible during the AC simulations and assignments. "Critical incidents" are the most effective means of achieving this. Dimensions and simulations are designed according to the critical incidents that are specific to a particular job. The process of gathering critical incidents produces descriptions of behaviour which form the basis of simulations. Dimensions and simulations are designed and constructed during the "work conference". Score lists and rating scales are also drawn up at this stage. They are designed to ensure that

Assessment Centres: A Practical Handbook. P. Jansen and F. de Jongh.
© 1997 John Wiley & Sons Ltd.

candidates receive the same treatment. The final stage of development is to check the AC's validity; does it achieve what it sets out to do?

5.2 WHAT IS A CRITICAL INCIDENT?

A critical incident is a situation of exceptionally effective or exceptionally ineffective behaviour, which is decisive for the achievement of key targets within an organisation.

Example: An organisation is involved in a project. Due to external influences, work falls behind schedule. A project manager makes up for lost time by reorganising the project. In this way he produces a positive critical incident. A sales person, however, who unknowingly snubs an important client which results in them taking their custom elsewhere, produces a negative critical incident.

Critical incidents should define concrete behaviour, describe exactly what a candidate did during an assignment. This behaviour should be distinguished separately from personal characteristics, the characteristics of an organisation or a candidate's thoughts and ideas. Behaviour is that which is visible and can be stimulated and measured during a simulation.

An effective critical incident not only provides a concrete description of behaviour, but also clearly demonstrates exceptionally effective or ineffective behaviour. To give us an idea of the effectiveness of behaviour, we need to determine the following; the purpose of the behaviour, which circumstances make this type of behaviour possible and the results that are achieved. A list of aims and results should be drawn up, to check if the final result corresponds with the aim. Sometimes aims and results differ from one another. A football player, for example, may dribble the ball past an opponent to go on and score a goal. He may also outplay an opponent in order to intimidate him and go on to score a goal much later on. It is also important to know which circumstances make certain responses possible. If an opponent had been outplayed by many different players before the player in question tackled him, his goal would be less conspicuous.

A critical incident consists of a total picture of cause, response and effect. The contents of a critical incident should be clearly observable and easy to verify. During an actual AC, an assessor will be expected to observe and evaluate causes, responses and effects. He can only observe a candidate's thoughts, for example, if they are translated into concrete actions.

5.3   GATHERING CRITICAL INCIDENTS

A job analysis can be made in the following ways:

- determine the job's place in the organisation scheme
- determine which tasks the job involves
- determine what type of demands a job involves
- determine how an employee is rewarded for effective job performance.

We know from experience that the critical incident method gives the best results for determining effective job performance. Employees who are asked to give information about a job are not used to thinking in terms of critical incidents, but in terms of a job's place within an organisation, its demands and the tasks it involves. In these cases, a special technique known as the *critical incident interview* is used.

The interview should focus on gathering examples of behaviour. It is, however, important to have some idea of what an organisation sets out to achieve and the sorts of situations it has to deal with. The interviewer should also have a global idea of the job's place within the organisation, its tasks and demands. Interviewers should make sure that the interview is not dominated by the listing of these aspects. The best way to do this is to ask for documentation and a job description beforehand.

The core of a critical incident interview is to ask starting questions which will trigger off more specific questions. During the preparations, interviewers should have armed themselves with an assortment of starting questions, for example:

- What is the difference between an effective . . . and a less effective . . .?
- Consider someone who is good at the job. What distinguishes him/her from the rest?
- What do you have to do to excel in this job?
- What would be the easiest way for someone in this job to cause damage to the company?

Starting questions usually produce descriptions of situations and behaviours. Informers often refer to vague characteristics like "stamina". These responses can be made more concrete by asking simple questions like "in what way is stamina shown?" The interviewer should pursue this line of questioning to get a total picture of a critical incident. Further specific questions can be:

- What did the person do exactly?
- What made you aware of this?

The interviewer should ask the following questions to get a better idea of what caused certain behaviour:

- What was the aim of this behaviour?
- What was wrong with the previous situation?
- What types of restrictions were put on behaviour?
- How was behaviour made easier than before?

An interviewer can get a better idea of the results of certain behaviour by asking the following questions:

- What happened as a result of this behaviour?
- In what way were the results evident?
- What would have happened if this person had not acted in this way; had taken another line of action?

The aforementioned questions will not fit every situation, which means that interviewers have to be able to adapt their questions. The interviewer should pursue questioning until cause, behaviour and effect can be defined in concrete terms. If the interviewer is satisfied, he may ask other starting questions such as "Do you know of another example?" A critical incident interview usually takes an hour, out of which three-quarters of an hour are dedicated to these cycles of starting questions, followed by more specific questions.

In many cases, the interview does not provide a totally concrete picture of a critical incident. However, it is essential to make a note of these "incomplete" incidents, since they can also contribute to the construction of an AC. It is advisable to use two interviewers per informer. One can concentrate upon the actual interviewing whilst the other makes notes. Finally, general interview techniques deserve some attention. The most important aspects are; try not to talk too often, interrupt as little as possible, ask open questions. Interviewers can also encourage informers to be more specific by using interjections like, "yes, hmmm" and silences. The interviewer should use a suitable mix of neutral questions and those that require a specific answer.

5.4   THE WORK CONFERENCE

Real development begins once the critical incidents have been gathered. Dimensions should be selected and made operational. Next, a list of instructions should be made for candidates, assessors and role-players. Score books have to be compiled for the In-basket and Memorandum assignments. Furthermore, a rating scale should be made for each practical assignment. These aspects can be developed effectively during the work conference.

A work conference lasts two days. A group of key figures acting on behalf of the organisation and a group of advisors carrying out the AC, take part in this conference. Obviously, the conference area should have the necessary equipment, PCs, photocopiers etc. It is also useful to have records of previous assignments and rating scales at hand.

The time available can be divided into units of four hours. At the start of each unit a meeting is held, during which work is designated and problems discussed. Work can be carried out individually or in groups of two. Two people should be given the task of compiling dimensions, while the rest concentrate on the development of assignments. When the dimensions are complete, work can be made on the rating scales. The development of the In-basket assignment involves the most work, not only because there are many items to invent, but also because the composition of the evaluation manual is very time consuming. This task is usually reserved for the persons representing the contracting organisation. They usually have the best information about the appropriate way in which to deal with In-basket items.

The work conference method has several advantages. The first draft of an AC can be compiled in a very short time. This demands a great deal of involvement from the advisors and the contracting organisation. Various aspects of the AC can be discussed and adjusted as much as the participants deem necessary. Alternative methods do not allow as much time for lengthy discussions.

5.5   SCORE LISTS AND RATING SCALES

If we measure something, there is always some doubt as to whether the measurement corresponds exactly with performance. Speedometers, for example, often register a higher speed than the actual speed that is being driven. This type of discrepancy also occurs in the measurement and assessment of human behaviour. Decisions are made on the basis of an AC which have far-reaching consequences for someone's career. Obviously, such discrepancies should not lead to the wrong decisions being made. Just as in the case of technical measuring instruments, errors in the assessment of human behaviour can be reduced to an acceptable level. One way of avoiding mistakes is to use more than one assessor for each candidate. Research has proven that assessments carried out by two assessors result in a significant increase in the assessment's reliability. Another way of avoiding mistakes is to instruct assessors carefully on how to determine which behaviour should be evaluated negatively or positively.

A score list is a checklist which includes examples of behaviour. For example, if a candidate comes across an anonymous complaint about an employee with a drink problem during an In-basket assignment, and responds by making an inquiry, the candidate will be given a positive score for the dimension entitled "problem-solving". If a candidate decides to take disciplinary action without conducting an investigation first, the candidate will receive a low score for the dimensions "problem-solving" and "interpersonal sensitivity". If a candidate delegates an investigation, at the same time keeping a watchful eye on the proceedings, the candidate will receive a positive score for "delegation and management control". During the construction of score lists critical incidents give a clear indication of what sort of behaviour is desirable or undesirable. Assessors use ticks to denote what type of behaviour candidates have demonstrated. The total score is made simply by adding up the ticks. A detailed score list ensures that assessors can arrive at satisfactory agreements.

The most common answers together with an evaluation are included in the score list. This will probably undergo a dramatic increase after a few ACs. The checklist will never become exhaustive, however. Participants are likely to come up with solutions that were not foreseen during the work conference or else did not occur during practice sessions. Sometimes instructions can be too rigid. They may, for example, stipulate that behaviour that is not shown on the list should be given a low score. In this way useful and original solutions are undervalued. This leads to frustration among assessors and, if there are great differences in the originality of solutions put forward by candidates, to systematic measuring mistakes. The score list is an effective means of sharpening observation and registering what an assessor has observed. It can form the basis of evaluating behaviour. However, as a decisive assessment instrument it offers assessors very few possibilities to draw on their professional skills and inside knowledge (see Chapter 7).

The rating scale is the most frequently used method for indicating the evaluation of behaviour. The assessors are allowed to give a candidate a maximum of seven points on each dimension. During assessor training they are informed which type of behaviour should receive what type of score. Chapter 8 includes an example of how the rating scale for the dimension "interpersonal sensitivity" in the Dialogue assignment can be filled in. The scale consists of four aspects of interpersonal sensitivity; "denial of someone's thoughts and feelings and acting out of self-interest", "being able to listen", "letting someone else talk" and "patience". The assessor has to consider all four aspects, but has considerable freedom to determine if the behaviour was sufficiently represented. Behaviour will differ in value according to which aspects it relates to. Assessors are left to weigh up the various aspects and arrive at a final score.

The rating scale allows assessors more room for interpretation and personal input than a score list. Sufficient training is required so that assessors can reach a consensus of opinion. During training, assessors become familiar with common assessment errors and how to avoid them. They should come to an agreement on what type of behaviour is desired or undesirable in an organisation. If assessors are from top management they will certainly have concrete ideas on this, but they may not always agree with one another.

5.6 CONTENT VALIDATION OF THE ASSIGNMENTS

The last step in the development of ACs consists of checking if the AC achieves what it sets out to do; ie checking its validity. Checks should be made on the simulations, the dimensions and the actual rating scales. These checks should be carried out in collaboration with the contracting organisation.

It is possible to design tailor-made simulations that correspond exactly with job situations. They should be based on the critical incidents that the job would entail. Tailor-made simulations encourage participants to accept the AC, because it is easy to make them see that they are being assessed on relevant behaviour. More obviously, the more accurate and well-constructed the simulation, the more effective the predictions.

There are various ways of checking if the contents of an AC correspond with the vacant job. Documents based on the job and reports from interviews provide information about what behaviour should be expected from the candidate. In addition, a representative group of employees may be consulted to evaluate the accuracy of the simulation. During training, assessors practice working with simulations and assessment techniques. Some assessors may find that simulations are not representative, or have difficulties with the assessment guidelines. Even at this stage, this type of criticism may result in adjustments being made, to ensure the AC's maximum validity.

Tailor-made simulations are costly if only a few candidates are being assessed for a certain function. From the point of view of cost-effectiveness it is advisable to opt for simulations that can be used for various jobs. Obviously a check would have to be made for every new function, to ensure that the standard assignments deal with relevant critical incidents and are representative for the job. This is necessary for the candidate's acceptance of the assignment and reliable predictions.

As was mentioned in Chapter 2, there are some doubts about the validity of assessing the performance of candidates on dimensions using several assignments. Dimensions, however, give an indication of the management qualities that are specific to a situation and should be demonstrated in several assignments. The management qualities relevant to a specific job should be stimulated during a satisfactory number of assignments. That is why it is useful to find out which assignments stimulate which dimensions. The number of times that the various dimensions are assessed should globally correspond with the importance that organisations lend to these dimensions.

The third step in checking an AC's validity is to take a careful look at the rating scales. In the case of pre-set rating scales and checklists, AC developers should find out if positively assessed performance during simulations would be given the same score within the organisation. For example, some organisations encourage employees to stand up for their own opinions, whereas other organisations may have very different thoughts on this matter. Furthermore, company spokesmen may air different opinions from those that are generally accepted by the department involved in the assessment proceedings. To ensure AC validity, constructors should be very critical in situations like these.

5.7 CONCLUSION

Critical incidents are indispensable for the development and validation of Assessment Centres. They provide the basis for simulations, the basis for determining the importance of dimensions and the basis for assessment aids like score lists and rating scales. Critical incidents guarantee valid simulations which candidates and assessors can easily recognise and relate to. The technical side of AC development demands well-conducted critical incident interviews, the structured integration of critical incidents in assignments and a feasible structuring of the evaluation process. The AC's ability to provide effective predictions is entirely dependent upon this type of expertise.

PART 3
The Assessment Centre Process

Chapter 6

Role-play in Dialogues

W. Vogtschmidt

6.1 THE DIALOGUE

The assignment known as the "Dialogue" forms an essential part of the Assessment Centre (see Chapter 3). A Dialogue is a simulation. It consists of a discussion between a candidate and a role-player. During the Dialogue candidates are presented with a range of issues that they are expected to confront and solve. The interaction between role-player and candidate stimulates certain responses from the candidate, which reveal important information about the candidate's capacities. This information is matched with the relevant criteria and given a score by the assessors.

The direct interaction that the Dialogue involves, results in the disclosure of key information about candidates that was not evident, or only partially evident during previous assignments. The role-player should create situations that stimulate candidates to behave in ways that are easy to evaluate. This chapter focuses upon the role-player's behaviour, attitude and function within the Dialogue and role-play training.

Assessment Centres: A Practical Handbook, P. Jansen and F. de Jongh.
© 1997 John Wiley & Sons Ltd.

6.2 MEASURING BEHAVIOUR IN DIALOGUES

During the Dialogue, candidates' behaviour should be visible and explicit, so that assessors can give them a score on dimensions. Thoughts and considerations are not visible and can not be given a score. Furthermore, the role-player has to get the candidate to display a wide range of behaviour, so that all the dimensions can be evaluated. He/she should ensure that differentiations can be made between successful and less successful performances within a dimension. In order to do this, the role-player should know what effective role-play comprises of.

6.3 CONCEPTS FOR ROLES IN DIALOGUES

A Framework for Role-play

Role-play versus Play-acting

The role-play is often associated with play-acting. Although role-playing and play-acting share some similarities, they do differ from one another. In a Dialogue role-players not only have to give a convincing rendition of a character but are also closely involved in the assessment process – they are part of a larger instrument. Role-playing and play-acting are both simulations of reality which involve, among other things, emotions and non-verbal behaviour. Just like an actor, a role-player has to portray a character. Both role-playing and play-acting require a lot of practice. In play-acting, actors receive directions from a director and refer to a script which contains clearly-defined behaviour. Timing is important and fellow actors usually know what is going to happen next. In role-play, however, the script consists of very global outlines, because conversations can always take different turns. The role-player only has a very general idea of what will happen because the candidate's input is obviously not predetermined.

The Role-player's Position

The role-player's reactions to a candidate should be kept within a clearly defined framework. Their task is to create a situation

within a particular setting which enables candidates to demonstrate their abilities in various dimensions, so that assessors can
give them scores on criteria. Role-players should aim to be as
consistent as possible so that all candidates receive the same
treatment.

The Double Role

Role-players have a double role in the Dialogue. They have to
respond naturally to the candidate as well as maintaining an
overview and gently guiding the course of the proceedings. This
is known as "process control". Their other task consists of helping candidates who are confused about their role instructions, to
get back on the right track. The role-player's main task is to
ensure that assessors can carry out the job of assessment. This is
obviously impossible if conversations reach a standstill. In this
case a role-player would be expected to intervene and try to
stimulate responses which could be evaluated. Effective process
control consists of creating favourable conditions for the candidate as well as the assessor. The candidate should be able to
express himself and the assessors should be supplied with relevant behaviour. This happens when the role-player offers "platforms" and responds to the candidate's platforms.

Platforms

To explain what is meant by the term "platform", a short excur-
sion will be made into the world of show-business. Everyone
can think of a comic duo consisting of a clown and a feed. The
feed's job is to help the clown to make a joke or to play a comic
scene. This is a very old and effective method. It is wrong to
think that the clown does all the work. Without the feed, the joke
would have less impact and probably would not even be
noticed. In a similar way to comic duos, Dialogues include
someone who acts as a feed – the role-player. He has to create
situations in which candidates can show their "tricks". In the
Dialogue these situations are known as "platforms". The role-
player can supply numerous "platforms" during the Dialogue.
Just like the feed, it is not his job to fill in these situations but to
leave them empty. A "platform" is, therefore, only a form, as
opposed to a hint, which stimulates specific behaviour. A candidate can also supply platforms by introducing a new theme or

subject. In this case the candidate is usually the first to fill in the platform. The role-player should respond accordingly.

The platform concept is formulated to give role-players more insight into the process of "feeding" during Dialogues. It is a tool. The use of this tool should lead to better communication and reciprocity between role-players, directors and assessors. However, some find the term "platform" ambiguous. Common alternatives are theme, point of departure, feed, aspect and hint. "Platform", however, embraces all these terms and does not conjure up any particular associations. This is what makes "platform" such an appropriate term, although there is no fixed definition for the term. In the Dialogue, the aspects which fall within the term "platform" consist of: a central problem that candidates have to resolve during the Dialogue, and the various themes related to this; the character portrayed by the role-player; the candidate's behaviour and the criteria which the candidate will be assessed upon etc. The concept behind platforms is to bring the process of "feeding" (guiding and manipulating the course of the Dialogue) into perspective. The role-player's main concern is to know how to feed, how to phrase feeds and when to supply them. Platforms, however, can only provide the role-player with an indication, there are no set rules.

It is understandable that some people find the term "platform" ambiguous. The term's lack of transparency is, however, quite constructive. It forces role-players to become more aware of the complexities involved in feeding ideas and guiding the course of conversations within a Dialogue. A platform can be seen, on the one hand, as a theme, and on the other hand, as a process or starting point. Themes and situations should be interpreted generally. In the first case, themes should be supplied by the role-player as well as the candidate. Themes or situations can relate to the emotional or relational aspects of the Dialogue. A remark, a comment, a gesture or the role-player's facial expression can also be seen as a platform or starting point. The themes which are dealt with during the conversation are based on role-instructions and determine the contents of the platforms. Naturally, candidates will come up with themes, processes and situations which are not included in the assignment's instructions.

The candidate's personality and attitude influences the type of platforms that the role-player supplies. If the candidate has a businesslike approach, then the role-player will introduce social aspects into the Dialogue, and vice versa. The role-player who is engaged in process control can also refer to the assessment dimensions for an idea of appropriate approaches. The dimensions should only be used as general guidelines, since the assignment's instructions and the candidate's behaviour are the main determinants for role-play. There is no direct correspondence between platforms and dimensions. The role-player can, however, present specific platforms that stimulate candidates to express dimension-related behaviour. In this case, the role-player should avoid being over-directive and hinting at the type of behaviour that is required.

The Role-player's Profile

What makes a good role-player? The role-player's personality determines how the role-player will behave during the Dialogue. The assignment instructions, however, also stipulate how the role-player should behave, so there is some tension between the two. The role-player, therefore, should be someone who is able to play a convincing role despite this complexity. Obviously, not everyone is cut out for this. But what are the psychological requirements for a successful role-player?

The role-player should:

- be able to identify with the candidate's situation;
- be able to identify with the role;
- be a good listener;
- be flexible and know how to react in unexpected situations;
- know how to keep the emotional level of a situation in the right balance;
- have a constant overview of the situation;
- remain constantly alert and assertive;
- give the appropriate level of guidance;
- make sure that verbal and non-verbal communication conform with one another;
- remain realistic and credible.

The role-player should not:

- be timid or loud;
- be someone who has difficulties in coping with unexpected situations;
- be someone who cannot help forming judgements about candidates;

- dominating and tending to steer the conversation in one direction;
- lose sight of the situation and miss opportunities that could help a candidate to express his/her abilities.

Dealing with Platforms

Platforms should be "empty" when they are presented to candidates, so that candidates are able to interpret them in their own way. The art is to divulge as little as possible. During a Dialogue, role-players may present certain platforms more than once, because some candidates fail to interpret platforms. This is where the better candidates distinguish themselves. They will quickly come forward with all sorts of relevant ideas, they will lead the conversation, want and be able to approach issues in various ways. Less able candidates need more encouragement and have to be supplied with more platforms, more frequently. At the beginning of a conversation or a new subject, the role-player should restrict prompting to a minimum, so that differences can be seen between those who are either quick or slow on the uptake. More encouragement can be used with slower candidates.

To ensure that candidates receive fair treatment a decision should be made on how far the role-player should go in prompting a candidate, and which platforms should have a standard place in the Dialogue. The platforms which are most relevant obviously should be put forward by the role-player. The role-player should make sure that the conversation does not dwell too long on one platform. Not all of the platforms that are important to the role-player as "boss" are as relevant to the candidate as "employee" and vice versa. Most importantly, the candidate should be allowed to show as many capacities as possible so that the assessors are able to give all dimensions a score.

Role-players should actively change over to another platform, if they feel that the platform has been dealt with long enough and that no more new information about the candidate's ability is being brought to light. If assessors want to know whether a candidate has more to offer, the role-player should put forward a more challenging platform. The same can be achieved by further questioning. If a candidate responds to this situation effectively and adopts a successful line of action, it can result in a higher score in one or more of the dimensions.

6.4 ROLE-PLAY TRAINING

Aims

Role-play training should aim at teaching role-players to create situations that allow candidates to demonstrate a wide range of abilities, so that assessors can assess them on relevant dimensions.

Training Scheme

The training programme should be based on the following: the person playing the role, the character of the role, what the role entails, and process control. Furthermore, it is useful to study the dimensions and the anchors used within the dimensions. The programme should train role-players so that they have no doubts about how the Dialogue should be conducted. The role-player should be well prepared and have the ability to empathise in order to play the part in a realistic and credible way. Obviously, sufficient practice in the various aspects of the role is also essential.

Before the role can be carried out in an actual Dialogue, the role-player should study the role as well as the assignment instructions very carefully.

- Phase 1: role analysis
- Phase 2: platform inventory
- Phase 3: train for the role

Phase 1

Training can begin with a discussion of how a role-player should behave in order to play his role effectively. Patterns of behaviour should be observed separately from the specific role (see section 6.3, Profile role-player). When a clear picture has been formed about what role-playing entails, the specific contents of the role can be determined.

A psychological profile of the role-play character should be made so that the role-player can identify with the part and have some idea of how the person would react in different situations. When analysing a part, it is best to start by making a list of the information that is included in the role-player's and candidate's instructions. Then the role-players should try to answer such questions as: "What type of social skills does the character have? How does he behave in a professional capacity? What do others think of him? What are his underlying motives? What sort of opinions does he hold?" and so on. At the end of Phase 1 a profile of the underlying role can be made.

Phase 2

When an inventory of available information has been made, we move on to Phase 2, the "platforms". What are the possible platforms? What themes can be brought up within a role (see section 6.3, Platform)? Which platforms should be put forward by the role-players, when, and in what way? It is also useful to ask "Which platform first? Which platform are we dealing with now? Should we go on to the next platform? How should we do that? Which platforms can a candidate put forward? Should I prompt the candidate? How should I do that, and how often? Should I be passive?" etc, etc. There are divided opinions on how often role-players should hint at platforms. Role-players should come to some sort of agreement on this. Restrictions could be put on duration, for example, if the candidate fails to respond to a platform after 10 minutes, the role-player should give a hint. Restrictions can also be put on quantity and frequency. For example, the role-player should give a maximum of three hints about the underlying problem and if the candidate still fails to respond, the role-player should leave it at that. In this case the role-player is presented with an important choice: should he/she choose not to give further hints, or try to make the problem emerge?

Timing is essential. A role-player may, for example, present a rather skeletal platform at a moment when the candidate is still processing information. The candidate may fail to register this and be given a low score as a result. But is this fair? We could say that the candidate has not been given a fair chance. The candidate might not have heard what had been said or failed to register the role-player's non-verbal sign. Good timing is, therefore, crucial. In Phase 2 the role-players should have fixed agreements on platforms and the approach they will adopt during the Dialogue.

Phase 3

Following the intensive analysis of the previous phases, the actual training for the role can begin. Since it is quite difficult to play the role in one go, it is advisable to train for the various phases which take place during the conversation. Video-recordings of the practice sessions are a very useful aid. The first stage of training consists of short, frequent sessions during which role-players learn the "right way" to present platforms. The length of the sessions is gradually increased. At the end of training, role-players take part in conversations lasting 20 minutes. The role-players are swapped over every five minutes. Each role-player elaborates on the part played by the previous trainee. This stage is seen as a very useful and constructive means of forming a total picture of the role.

Chapter 7

The Assessment of Written Assignments

F.D. de Jongh

7.1   INTRODUCTION

All the practical assignments that are used in Assessment Centres are designed to stimulate and evaluate relevant, observable behaviour. Relevant behaviour is determined by the choice of dimensions. Experienced AC designers can come up with ideas for observable behaviour fairly easily. These ideas are put to the test during try-outs.

A successful AC stimulates candidates to display observable behaviour as much as possible. This behaviour is then assessed. It is the subject of assessment that this chapter deals with, focusing upon the assessment of written assignments such as the In-basket and Memorandum.

7.2   ASSESSMENT

The assessment of candidates during practical assignments follows a standard pattern:

Assessment Centres: A Practical Handbook, P. Jansen and F. de Jongh.
© 1997 John Wiley & Sons Ltd.

- observing
- making notes
- classifying
- quantifying
- evaluating
- reporting.

Observing and Making Notes

During oral assignments, assessors observe candidates and make a report of what they see and hear. These reports should be as written in a literal manner. During the assessment of written work, assessors read the material and make notes on a checklist.

Classifying

The notes that were made during observation have to be transferred to the behaviour anchored rating scales and written under the dimension categories. This process is known as classifying.

Quantifying

Five- or seven-point rating scales are used in the AC. In the five-point scale, a score of five points indicates optimal behaviour, a score of three points indicates acceptable behaviour and a score of one point indicates least successful behaviour. The seven-point scale goes from seven to four to one and is otherwise exactly the same as the five-point scale. When assessors have determined what type of behaviour belongs to which dimension, they have to decide which score they should give. The texts which are included in the rating scales give some guidelines on this. In this way, each dimension is evaluated per assignment. The assessment is both qualitative – accompanied by a short text, and quantitative – given a score.

7.3   ORAL AND WRITTEN ASSIGNMENTS

Both written and oral assignments are carried out during an AC. Assessors are present during oral assignments, but not during written assignments. The former are usually evaluated by company assessors. Sometimes written assignments are evaluated by external AC advisors.

7.4   THE ASSESSMENT OF WRITTEN ASSIGNMENTS

The assignment known as the "In-basket" is the most well-known written assignment. The Memorandum and Fact-finding assignments are also very common. The assessment of In-basket assignments is based on the candidate's written response to the assignment. Sometimes interviews are used to supplement the assessment.

In-basket

There are many different types of In-baskets. Since all managers have to deal with post, an In-basket can be developed for every type of management job. As a rule, it is fairly easy to come up with the type of notes, memos, telephone messages and so forth that one would usually find in a manager's in-tray. Interviews with several managers also provide sufficient material on this. It is more difficult to determine what the correct reaction to the various items in the in-tray should be. This should be determined in the developmental stage, before the assignment is carried out. This usually takes place as follows. Once the choice of items has been made for the In-basket, managers who are active in the same area should be asked to comment on the assignment and say what they feel would be the best response to the various In-basket items. Their answers are used to compose a checklist.

There are two types of checklists; detailed and global. The detailed checklist includes detailed specifications of what should be expected from a candidate. The global checklist consists of more general outlines. Many feel tempted to opt for the detailed method; determining whether a reaction is good or bad might appear very easy if one had a list of standardized reactions to refer to. It is a simple and fairly reliable method, but some doubt its validity. A candidate may, for example, react in a way that had not been prescribed, but is just as appropriate. In the detailed method (see Figure 7 1) a reaction of this kind would be ignored or given a negative score.

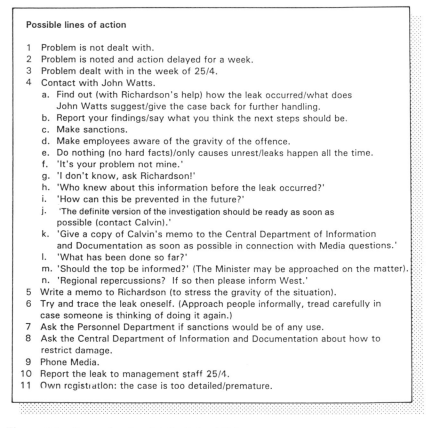

Possible lines of action

1 Problem is not dealt with.
2 Problem is noted and action delayed for a week.
3 Problem dealt with in the week of 25/4.
4 Contact with John Watts.
   a. Find out (with Richardson's help) how the leak occurred/what does John Watts suggest/give the case back for further handling.
   b. Report your findings/say what you think the next steps should be.
   c. Make sanctions.
   d. Make employees aware of the gravity of the offence.
   e. Do nothing (no hard facts)/only causes unrest/leaks happen all the time.
   f. 'It's your problem not mine.'
   g. 'I don't know, ask Richardson!'
   h. 'Who knew about this information before the leak occurred?'
   i. 'How can this be prevented in the future?'
   j. 'The definite version of the investigation should be ready as soon as possible (contact Calvin).'
   k. 'Give a copy of Calvin's memo to the Central Department of Information and Documentation as soon as possible in connection with Media questions.'
   l. 'What has been done so far?'
   m. 'Should the top be informed?' (The Minister may be approached on the matter).
   n. 'Regional repercussions? If so then please inform West.'
5 Write a memo to Richardson (to stress the gravity of the situation).
6 Try and trace the leak oneself. (Approach people informally, tread carefully in case someone is thinking of doing it again.)
7 Ask the Personnel Department if sanctions would be of any use.
8 Ask the Central Department of Information and Documentation about how to restrict damage.
9 Phone Media.
10 Report the leak to management staff 25/4.
11 Own registration: the case is too detailed/premature.

Figure 7.1 Example of a detailed checklist

A global checklist (see Figure 7.2) gives information on the types of direction that candidates should take, rather than precise lines of action.

When assessors use the detailed checklist they tend to arrive at similar scores. With this method it is not necessary to use managers as assessors; this task can be carried out by psychological assistants, for example. With the global checklist, however, managers have to be used, or experienced senior-consultants who know what would be expected of managers in these types of situations.

Procedure for Assessing an In-basket

First, the material has to be read. Then the candidate's reactions are compared with those on the checklist and noted down. If the

PROBLEM ANALYSIS	Find out how this could have happened and who should be informed quickly about what the investigation will entail. Check how this can be avoided in the future. Find out political consequences.
PROBLEM SOLVING	Start an investigation into the causes of the incident. Inform the relevant people involved and prepare them for questions from the outside. Organise prevention.
SOCIABILITY	Inform colleagues who might be asked questions by the media.
DELEGATING AND MANAGEMENT CONTROL	Ask Watts to trace the leak and report his findings. Secretary is given the task of informing those concerned.
PLANNING AND ORGANISING	Work fast.

Figure 7.2 Example of a global checklist

candidate's reaction is very similar to the checklist, this will be given a high score. The more the candidate's reactions deviate from the checklist, the lower the score. The assessor writes down a score and comment on a survey form, and organises the candidate's reactions into dimensions. The completion of the checklist and the survey form is the first stage of assessment known as "Observation and making notes" (see Figure 7.3). After this, the rating scales should be filled in. The assessor has to make an assessment on each dimension. This is done with the help of the information included in the survey form. A final score should be reached by looking at the trend of the scores per dimension rather than calculating the mean average.

The candidate's use of available time should also be taken into consideration. If a candidate fails to deal with all the items within the time limit, this should only affect the dimension "Planning and Organising". As for the other dimensions, assessors should look at the quality of a candidate's approach.

The assessment of an In-basket should result in a score and a comment per dimension. This should be done by two assessors. A director compares the scores and if the score per dimension differs by more than two points, he will ask the assessors to resolve this difference between them. The assessors can easily identify which dimensions differ in score by referring to the survey form. When they have come to an agreement, they inform the director about it.

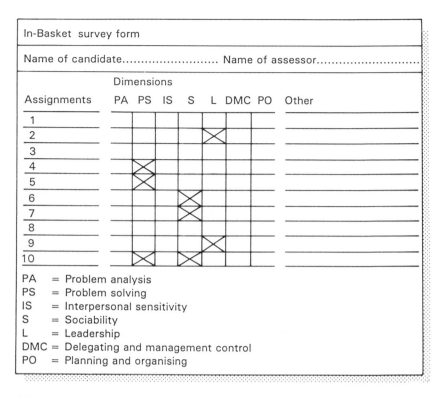

Figure 7.3 Example of an In-basket survey form

Memorandum

Most of the ACs that are used by the Government or other public authorities include one assignment which involves the analysis of written material. This type of assignment is also used in AC's designed for larger profit-making concerns.

Like the In-basket, the Memorandum comes in several varieties. All assignments are based on a central theme but have different aims and are constructed in a different way. Sometimes candidates are asked to make a short policy document, or plan an approach or a project. This plan or document then has to be presented to a commission of assessors. In this case the assignment is referred to as an "Analysis" and a "Presentation" assignment. During the assessment of Analysis/ Presentation assignments, assessors should make sure that they do not assess written material separately from the oral presentation. This may result in a candidate being evaluated twice on the same dimension. Another version which involves the analysis of written material is the Memorandum draft. Candidates are expected to examine a draft for a memorandum written by a manager colleague, and suggest ways in which it could be improved.

This section concentrates on how written policy documents, strategy plans, project plans or comments on memorandum drafts can be assessed. The same line of approach that was used for the In-basket should be used here. As in the case of the In-basket, it is not difficult to find an interesting theme and devise assignments. It is, however, difficult to determine assessment norms. Furthermore, certain measures are made to make sure that candidates receive fair treatment, which also puts a limit on the number of options.

One might think that the easiest way to determine assessment norms would be to let as many managers as possible carry out the assignment and then draw up a list of assessment norms based on their findings. This is easier said than done; managers are not alike. An ingenious memorandum written by a very creative manager should not be used as the norm for average candidates. On the other hand, a more general memorandum should not be used as the norm for ingenious or creative candidates. As a result it is better to use global criteria for the assessment of candidate performance. The more specific the contents of the assignment, the greater the need for internal assessors.

The Memorandum is assessed in a similar way to the In-basket. The assessor goes through the assignment fairly globally, ticks off points on a checklist (see Figure 7.4) and transfers the notes to the rating scales. A director examines the assessments, looks for any discrepancies in the scores and decides if assessors should discuss certain scores. A note is made of the final scores, then all the information is included in a report.

Fact Finding

The assignment known as "Fact Finding" is quite similar to the Memorandum and the various separate items of the In-basket. The difference between Fact Finding and the other assignments is that Fact Finding is carried out in various stages and deliberately sets out to overload candidates with information which they then have to deal with in a short space of time.

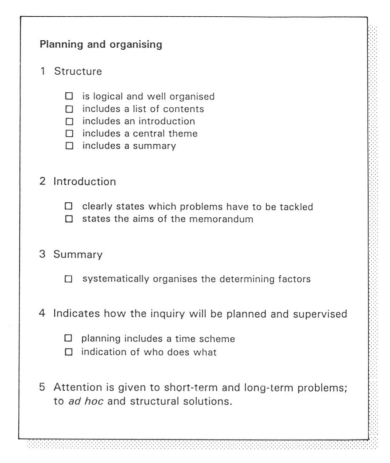

Figure 7.4 Example of a global checklist for the memorandum assignment – the dimension of planning and organising

A candidate may, for example, be presented with an application for building permission. The candidate is given a limited amount of information and is expected to make a decision. Once the candidate's written response is submitted, the candidate is bombarded with information and then asked to write and submit another one. In the third phase, additional information is supplied which either makes it necessary to inform a superior of the decision and/or undertake another line of action. Candidates are then asked to carry this out. The actual decision is not the main focus of interest but the procedures that the candidate follows and the considerations included in the written response.

The method which is used to assess Fact-finding assignments is quite similar to those used for the In-basket and

Memorandum. The Fact-finding assignment looks more specifically at whether the candidate's actions are appropriate (in the eyes of the contractor). Fact-finding assignments are usually tailor made and there are many possible variants. This means that the assessment of Fact-finding assignments cannot rely too heavily on checklists or rating scales. It is impossible to determine criteria for standard reactions since the candidate's possibilities are endless. The assessors have to rely on their own expertise. That is why internal assessors are used in Fact-finding assignments.

When all the candidates have completed the Fact-finding assignment, the assessors take part in an evaluation session. This consists of them reading all the candidates' assignments, which gives them an overall picture of the types of performance and actions. Assessors should avoid regarding the average performance as the average norm; all the candidates, for example, may have performed worse than the contractor had expected. The norm can be determined or adjusted during a short discussion. After the reading session, candidates' work is shared out among the assessors. Two assessors are assigned to each candidate. The assessment is carried out according to the previously discussed method (see section 7.2) and deals with all three phases of the candidate's work.

The final assessment is reliable because during the evaluation session, assessors discuss differences in scores. This method could also be applied to the Memorandum assignment, in the case of standardisation of a newly developed complex instrument, for example.

7.5   ELECTRONIC ASSESSMENT TECHNIQUES

The assessment of In-baskets and Memoranda is very time-consuming. The use of company managers for assessment would involve an extra day per manager. If the company employed external advisors it would cost a lot of money. There are various ways of solving these problems. The more detailed scoring system which allows less expensive assessors to be used has already been discussed. The temptation to use one assessor instead of two is also great. Another option would be to use an electronic testing system or interactive media. An electronic system could only be used in In-basket assignments, however. The assessment of Memorandum assignments will always remain manual. It might seem tempting to use an electronic system for the In-basket assignment; this would save four hours of assessment time. The main disadvantage is its form – multiple-choice questions are not interactive. This method leaves no room for initiative, creative solutions, decisive responses etc. The only aspects that could be assessed would be the candidate's ability to judge alternatives and how fast he or she can react. This does have some merit but is rather lightweight in comparison with the In-basket essay.

_____ Chapter 8

Directing during an Assessment Centre

F.D. de Jongh

8.1 THE DIRECTOR'S ROLE

Candidates are assessed by assessors in Assessment Centres. Assessors are guided, coached and supervised by directors, who are AC specialists. An Assessment Centre could be compared to a circus act: a perfect performance depends on the dedication and expertise of all those involved. Directors are like the ring-masters – at "le moment suprême" they are responsible for a perfect show.

Directors have many different tasks, but they should not take on everything. They should not work as assessors, role-players or test room leaders – nor should they see to catering or ensure that the AC programme runs on schedule. During large-scale ACs, it is very important for everyone to be assigned their own specific tasks and responsibilities, otherwise the reliability and validity of the ACs are thrown into question. Nearly all the evaluations of ACs that are submitted by assessors and

Assessment Centres: A Practical Handbook, P, Jansen and F. de Jongh.
© 1997 John Wiley & Sons Ltd.

candidates, reveal that smooth logistic management is just as important as an AC's face-validity.

Although assessors have been trained to observe and assess candidates, that does not rule out the risk of subjective judgements. That is why assessors are carefully and continuously monitored by AC specialists. Constant attention is given to their assessments and the type of observations that they are based on.

During an AC the director has to perform the following tasks:

- receive, guide and, if necessary, reassure the candidate
- monitor procedures
- ensure that procedures are followed correctly
- set an example to the assessors
- act as a chairperson
- give feedback to role-players, if necessary.

8.2   CANDIDATE GUIDANCE

Candidates are often nervous, even though every effort is made to prepare them for an Assessment Centre. Sometimes information sessions are held beforehand, which are also a form of training. All candidates are provided with information brochures which give comprehensive descriptions of the procedures, dimensions and tasks that will be used in the AC. Nevertheless, some candidates remain apprehensive. Many people who are not well-acquainted with ACs often associate them with pitfalls, tricks and hidden agendas. This is definitely not what one should expect. The director should always keep an eye out for extremely nervous candidates, and notify the coordinator so that the candidate can be helped accordingly.

The director should also assist candidates during the Dialogue or Group Discussion. During the Presentation, the assessor acting as the delegation chairperson is usually responsible for candidates. The director is responsible for the seating arrangements for the Dialogue and the Group Discussion (this is dealt with in section 8.3). At the end of the AC, the director shows the candidate out. Once they have completed the assignments candidates usually have to return to the test room. If a candidate looks slightly dazed, help should be offered. For example, it may be very useful to refer to the AC schedule.

8.3   MONITORING THE PROCEDURE

The director should keep an eye on the time, arrange the seating in the performance rooms, set up the overhead projector, hand out and collect the necessary forms, notes, instructions etc and check the rating scales.

Time

The director should make sure that assignments begin and end on time, and that assessment discussions do not overrun otherwise they will have a disruptive effect on the AC. A stopwatch should be used for this purpose. On average, 10 minutes are reserved for giving scores and 10 minutes for discussion. The director should always have a programme close at hand to ensure that the various activities stay on schedule.

Seating

During the Dialogue, the Presentation and the Group Discussion candidates should be seated so that they can be well observed by assessors. This is the director's responsibility. Each assignment requires a different layout. Examples of these appear in Figure 8.1.

Overhead Projector

An overhead projector is often used during presentations. Some candidates think that being able to use an overhead projector is part of the test, but this is not the case. The director should make sure that the equipment is well set up and assist the candidate, if necessary. The director should also arrange the assessors' seats so that they are able to watch the screen *and* the candidate. The commission chairperson has the task of receiving the candidate as well as leading the discussion.

Papers

The director makes sure that each assessor receives a form for notes and a set of rating scales for each session. The director should count these beforehand to make sure that he has the required amount. If there are not enough, the coordinator

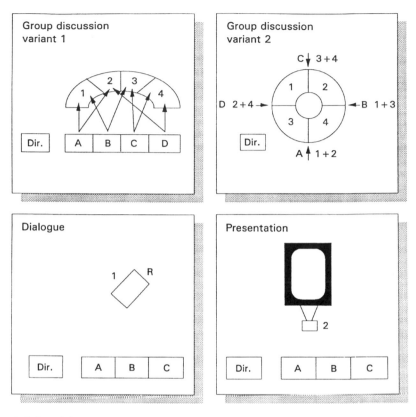

1,2,3 and 4 = candidates
R = role player
Dir. = director
A,B,C and D = assessor
Arrow = assessor assesses

Figure 8.1 Examples of seating layouts

should be informed. The director also makes sure that documents relating to the AC are not left behind in the performance rooms. Candidates should not receive any information about their assessment during the AC, or have AC materials in their possession. It is the responsibility of the coordinators, test room staff and directors to prevent this from happening. Disappearance of materials is considered as theft.

Survey of Results

The director fills in the survey of results (see Figure 8.2).

Assessment Centre				Confidential

Survey of results   **Dialogue**

Name of candidate ....

Date ....

Assessor A ....

Assessor B ....

Assessor C ....

Director ....

Management dimensions	A	B	C	average
Problem analysis				
Problem solving				
Interpersonal sensitivity				
Sociability				
Leadership				
Delegation and management control				
Firmness				
Resolution				

Figure 8.2   Survey of results for the dialogue

The scores given by the various assessors are written down on a survey form – preferably set horizontally. That is, the scores from all assessors should be noted for the first dimension, followed by all the scores for the second dimension, etc (see Figure 8.3). This is quicker than noting down all the scores for each assessor separately (vertically). Turning pages is time consuming and can lead to mistakes being made.

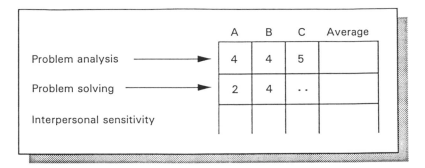

Figure 8.3 Example of how to fill in a survey of results

This method is straightforward. Differences in scores can be seen at a glance. The director indicates which dimensions differ more than two points from one another – these will have to be discussed with the assessors.

Exchange of Information

Information concerning candidates should not be exchanged during an AC. The director should set an example and make sure that assessors and role-players do not discuss candidates with each other or, more importantly, with the client or the person representing the client.

8.4   MODEL ASSESSOR

The seven point rating scale indicates what type of behaviour is desired in relation to a certain dimension during a certain assignment. Seven denotes optimal behaviour. One denotes the least successful behaviour. Four indicates average behaviour (see Figure 8.4).

In order to write an accurate report, it is very important for the rating scales to be filled in correctly. This is also crucial to the discussion of score differences between assessors, which often leads to adjustments being made. The director, however, should not make any assessments or give scores. For the purposes of the report, it is useful if the director supplements the rating scales, by underlining and adding comments. The director who attended the AC usually writes the reports.

The director's notes often act as a useful supplement to the rating scales. These notes can be indispensable, especially if an

Interpersonal sensitivity	Dialogue

7- Able to acknowledge the other person's thoughts and feelings and able to adapt his behaviour to this. Good listener. Lets the other person finish what he wants to say. Is patient.

6-

5-

4- Reasonably able to acknowledge the other person's thoughts and feelings. Sometimes a good listener, sometimes not. Lets the other person finish talking on the whole. Occasionally impatient.

3-

2-

1- Unable to acknowledge the other person's thoughts and feelings and adapt his behaviour to this. Condescending. Interrupts often. Is impatient.

Figure 8.4 Example of a rating scale

assessor failed to include any notes. Assessors do not have to write down what they observe word for word, but they should be as literal as possible. The length of texts differs per individual, some assessors give far more detailed accounts than others.

The director should set an example to the assessors. He or she should not criticise or praise the candidate before the AC's results are made known officially. Any comments or other indications should be nipped in the bud. Fortunately this rarely happens.

8.5   EXPERT ON THE ASSESSMENT CENTRE'S CONTENTS

Sometimes assessors are badly prepared and have not read the information brochure thoroughly. However, directors can expect all sorts of questions and should be able to provide accurate answers. A few examples of these are shown below.

Questions

The director might be asked questions on the AC programme (see Chapter 9). Assessors may not know where to report and at what time for a certain assignment. The director should know this, and should also be able to answer questions about assignments. Candidates tend to ask more questions about the Presentation than the Dialogue and the Group Discussion. Directors should know both the candidates' and the role-players' instructions. Questions are always asked – so directors should make sure that they are well prepared.

Expert on Dimensions

Directors should be experts on dimensions, so that they can check if assessors have classified behaviour under the right dimension. If this has not been done correctly, directors should correct the mistake and indicate which dimension the behaviour belongs to. Directors should always have a list of dimensions and the rating scale guide at hand.

Assessments

Strictly speaking, although directors should not give scores, there are a few exceptions. For example, when a discussion may have reached a deadlock situation. If a director decides to offer his opinion, he should support this with observation data rather than get involved in assessment. If one of the assessors is playing a win or lose game, this could seriously undermine the director's authority and put his other roles at stake.

Expert Judge at Assessment

The director should be an expert judge as far as assessment is concerned. He or she should be able to detect discrepancies and

Checklist of assessment tendencies

By using the checklist below you can check if your assessments follow a certain trend.

Halo

The tendency to allow a positive score on a dimension to carry on into other dimensions. You can check this by comparing your first scores with the rest. If there is hardly any difference between these and your scores are high, this could be an indication of a 'Halo'.

Horn

The reverse tendency. A negative score carries on into the other dimensions. You can check this in the same way as the 'Halo'.

Central tendency

The tendency to avoid extreme scores and stay within the middle range. This tendency occurs quite frequently if the seven point score system is being used. A series of four point scores are usually an indication of this effect. It is fairly easy to check.

Leniency

The tendency to give high scores. You can check this by comparing your own scores with the scores on the matrix. Are most of your scores sevens and eights?

Severity

The tendency to give below-average scores. If your scores are mainly ones and twos this may be the case.

Figure 8.5   Checklist of assessment tendencies

choose the right moment to discuss them. A director may, for example, refer to assessment tendencies and say "This seems like a halo – or leniency tendency." (see Figure 8.5).

Giving Feedback to Role-players

Role-players are consultants, co-workers of the client or actors. Even though they follow a thorough training, this does not imply that they always act correctly or know how to enact their role. The director has to comply with their wish for feedback. A few minutes can be reserved for this following an assignment, when the assessors are filling in the rating scales. The director has to decide whether the role-player has played the role consistently during a single session, or more sessions. It is crucial for the role-player to offer the candidate enough opportunities to demonstrate observable behaviour and get a score. The director should give feedback on this and say which changes, if any, are necessary.

8.6   CHAIRMAN OF DECISIVE MEETINGS

If scores differ two points or more, the director chairs a discussion between the assessors who were responsible for these scores. This is difficult if the assessors are not used to discussing their motives. One should not put too much emphasis on the scores; it is a waste of time to spend half an hour discussing respectively whether to change scores of two and six into two fours.

The aim of the discussion is to examine the reasons behind a particular decision. If assessors are willing to change scores on this basis, they will be convinced that the correction was positive and valid. The discussion should lead to a clear picture of the observations on which the scores are based and how much effect the different observations have had in determining the scores.

These types of discussions might result in:

• assessors discovering that their observations were selective;
• assessors discovering that they have mixed the same kind of behaviour with different dimensions, or that they have judged the same kind of behaviour differently.

These discussions are often pleasant and enriching. They usually result in well-founded and balanced judgements. Some people, however, disagree with this and want the discussions to be removed from the programme. They think that the director should intervene in the case of score differences. However, these discussions are often constructive and useful, and having to account for one's scores encourages assessors to be more accurate and attentive.

Procedure-orientated Chairing

The aim of these discussions is to arrive at a consensus of opinion on the observed behaviour and the assessments for each dimension. The way in which this takes place is just as important as what it sets out to achieve. The chairperson should make sure that the discussion follows a set procedure. The chairperson should not attempt to influence the course of the discussion. The director is nothing more than the discussion leader. His task is to find out which observations the assessments are based upon. The director should try to get full answers, summarise these answers and ask if this summary is correct, first by asking the assessors one by one and then as a group.

Opinion-forming

The process of adjusting value judgements can be regarded as opinion-forming. Assessors make a list of the types of behaviour on which the evaluation is based and clarify this. Then they try to arrive at the same conclusions, based on the behaviour that they observed. Even if this is successful, assessors may still adhere to their original scores. This may be due to them assessing the same type of behaviour differently, or due to one assessor putting more emphasis on positive behaviour while the other focuses on negative behaviour. The director should intervene and curtail such types of discussions.

Openness

Managers who are not prepared to listen to other people's opinions, or who won't change their opinions are not suitable for the job of assessor. This does not, however, occur very often. Once assessors are aware of the aims and effects of Assessment Centres, they are usually motivated to fit in with the AC's demands.

During the AC the director has to try to create an open atmosphere. The assessors should be stimulated to put forward their arguments and listen to others. In this way, assessors are forced to review their opinions. In this type of atmosphere the onus is upon establishing conformity rather than looking for disparity.

Consensus of Opinion

Assessors should try to arrive at a consensus of opinion. An inventory should be made of the different opinions and then examined. The director should.

- make an inventory
- clarify the inventory
- make a summary of the most important points
- check whether the summary is correct
- formulate an opinion that everyone agrees with.

Different Situations

The director's attitude during discussions depends on the type of situation that he finds himself in. Discussion situations have been divided into the following categories:

Harmony

This situation seems to be an ideal one. Assessors share similar opinions and try to arrive at an agreement together. This usually consists of looking for the highest common denominator. The director does not play a big role.

Conflict

In this situation opinions seem irreconcilable and assessors end up arguing about differences. Obviously, no-one can make a good decision in a situation like this. Any attempts to do so would be undermined and totally ineffective. In this situation both parties become less and less inclined to review or change their opinions. If the director tried to persuade them otherwise, the assessors would probably end up quarrelling with him. This would seriously undermine the director's authority and have negative consequences for his other roles. The only thing that the director can do in this situation is to ask for the observation data on which the assessments are based. He will then work out the average of these scores.

Coalition

Often different opinions seem to be in conflict with one another, but this is not always the case. Sometimes assessors are willing to work together to find a solution. To do this they must first agree on observation data. If the assessors are willing to come to an agreement and wish to avoid intervention then the following procedure could be followed:

- a clear list of existing opinions should be made and preferably backed up with visual material (survey of results on a flip-chart);
- a list of points on which assessors differ/agree should be made;
- investigate whether the points on which assessors agree can apply or be made to apply to everyone;
- negotiate on the differences: formulate by using the phrase "on the one hand/on the other hand" and take the average of the scores.

8.7 CONCLUSION

The director's job is difficult, fun and crucial. The director should ensure that the course of the AC is reliable and methodologically justified. This task should not be combined with other tasks like role-playing and assessing, for example.

If this job is done well:

- Candidates will be convinced that they received careful and honest treatment.
- Role-players will play consistently.
- Assessors will assess fairly.

Chapter 9

The Logistic Management of Assessment Centres

K. Geling

9.1 INTRODUCTION

Logistics play an essential role in the preparation and implementation of Assessment Centres. An Assessment Centre (AC) should run smoothly, any mistakes could affect the reliability of candidates' results. This chapter looks at the origin and meaning of the word "logistics" and deals with the logistic activities involved in the organisation of an AC, in which the programme plays a crucial role. Logistic management should always put candidates first and ensure that they are given the same chances in the same situations.

The Origin of the Word "Logistics"

In the *Collins English Dictionary* "logistics" is defined as:

1. The science of the movement, supplying, and maintenance of military forces in the field.

Assessment Centres: A Practical Handbook, P. Jansen and F. de Jongh.
© 1997 John Wiley & Sons Ltd.

2. The management of materials' flow through an organisation from raw materials to finished goods.
3. The detailed planning and organisation of any large complex operation. From French *logistique* from "loger" to "lodge".

The word logistics was first used by the French army during the reign of Louis XIV. They realised that the effectiveness of a military operation not only depended on the availability of weapons and soldiers but also on transportation and the supply of food and munitions. The management of transportation, the supplying of food, materials and men, as well as the management and control of supplies, was known as logistics.

What is Logistic Management?

Logistic management ensures that the right people, services and/or products are available at the right place at the right time. Logistics is, therefore, the logical planning and organisation of people, services and/or products, whether it is for the transportation of goods, production control or the organisation of an AC. Effective logistic management is essential for the preparation and execution of ACs. The employees who are involved in carrying out an AC have to be planned in at the right time for the tasks that they have been assigned. The various products that are used during the AC should also be delivered before a certain date.

9.2 THE INFORMATION REQUIRED FOR AN AC PROGRAMME

A number of facts have to be established before the AC programme can be written. It is important to know how many candidates are taking part in the AC. The AC's duration is dependent on the number of candidates, which can vary from one to 100. The number and type of assignments, oral or written, also influence the AC's duration and how the programme is put together. Candidates are given two to three hours for the completion of written assignments like the Memorandum and In-basket. The evaluation of this is usually carried out afterwards. The various oral assignments require preparation time, time in which to perform the assignment, and assessment time. Practice time is scheduled so that candidates can carry out the actual assignment in a performance room immediately afterwards. As soon as the candidate leaves the room, the candidate's performance is evaluated by the assessors under the direction of the director. This assessment time differs per assignment and can vary from 20 minutes to one hour. With this method only a limited number of candidates can be dealt with each day. In AC's consisting of more than four or five participants parallel groups have to be used as well as several performance rooms, so that more than one candidate can be evaluated at a time. The number of assessors depends on the number of candidates and assignments; two to three assessors per room being fairly standard. Some AC assignments such as the Dialogue require role-players. One or more role-players are also used in Group Discussions, depending upon the number of candidates taking part in the assignment.

9.3   THE PROGRAMME OR ASSESSMENT CENTRE TIMETABLE

The programme plays a central role in the AC's organisation. It could be compared to a train timetable, which contains exact information about departure and arrival times, connections and route networks. The AC programme contains similar information. It states who is doing what, where and at what moment in time. It includes a list of directors, role-players, assessors, test room staff, logistic coordinators, and their specific tasks and responsibilities. The names of all AC participants and staff are also listed in the programme book and assigned a personal code. A code is also used to denote the specific rooms that are used during the AC.

The AC programme should be organised so that all candidates are given the same chances in the same situations. Obviously, it should work well for everyone. The order of assignments, the interchanging of assessors, the duration of assignments, waiting times and possible additions to the programme should take this into account.

The Order of Assignments

Sometimes the Memorandum, which is written by candidates is used in the Presentation. This obviously affects the programme.

If a Presentation is only based on information given in the assignment instructions, it is not important whether the Presentation precedes the Memorandum or vice versa. It is important to think carefully about the order in which assignments take place. It is best to alternate oral and written assignments. Written assignments should be completed in one go, the In-basket being an exception. This assignment can be spread over two sessions of equal duration. This approach is justified if it reduces or else eliminates waiting times between assignments. After all, in real life it is highly unlikely for someone to be able to go through an in-tray undisturbed. In the case of oral assignments preparation time always precedes the actual performance. Finally, not all candidates are engaged in the same assignments at the same time.

Interchanging Assessors

A candidate should not be evaluated constantly by the same group of assessors. This is not too difficult to arrange, especially in AC's that use parallel groups, as assessors can be interchanged after each assignment. In this way, even though assignments take place in the same performance room, each candidate is evaluated by different assessors for each assignment. This system also caters for candidates who may or may not want to be evaluated by a particular assessor. Requests like this can be included in the programme. Candidates are also allowed to state their preferences regarding which candidates they participate with. Attempts should be made to honour such requests, for example a lunch made up of two or three sittings could be one solution.

Walking Times, Waiting Times and Lunchtime

The time needed by candidates and assessors to get from one assignment to another should be taken into account when compiling a programme. It is advisable to leave a space of five minutes between each assignment. Waiting times or breaks are inconvenient for candidates as well as assessors and should be avoided where possible. Not all candidates are able to carry out oral assignments at the same time. One way of reducing breaks like this is to spread written assignments over two shorter sessions. Finally, it is important to know at what times lunch can be held. In some cases lunch is restricted to certain times. Obviously allowances should be made for this in the programme.

Additional Items

In the case of large ACs the assessors and/or role-players receive (extra) instruction at the beginning of the AC from the director(s). The AC programme and the various assignments are also taken through here, and sufficient time should be reserved for this in the programme. At the end of the day an appraisal interview is held, during which candidates complete an evaluation form and talk to an assessor or coordinator about their experiences of each assignment. It is essential to ask candidates whether they felt that they were able to perform well, and which aspects, if any, they may have found negative or restricting. The organisational aspects of the AC are also dealt with during the interview.

AC programmes demand great precision. Even the smallest of errors will have repercussions on the AC. Imagine what sort of problems would arise if two candidates, for example, were scheduled to take part in the Dialogue assignment in the same room and at the same time! Taking previously mentioned guidelines into account, there are several different ways of compiling a programme. It is essential that the programme runs well for the candidates and does not include too many unnecessary breaks. Table 9.1 represents a section of an AC programme which is designed for twelve candidates and consists of five assignments.

9.4 THE COORDINATION PROGRAMME AND THE TEST ROOM SCHEDULE

Once the AC programme is complete, a coordination programme and a test room schedule can be made. The coordination programme contains a list of the coordinator's tasks during the AC. The coordinator's main job is to make sure that the logistic side of the AC runs smoothly: this consists of preparing files which contain a list of the assignments, preparing the performance areas, setting up the necessary audio visual equipment and material that the candidates will be assessed on, collecting completed assessment material and processing the

Table 9.1 Section of a programme

AC programme 29 January

Item	Time	Candidates	Assessors/directors	role-players	Room
Reception candidates	08.30–08.40	1–12		a b x	TR
Reception assessors	08.35–08.45		A to F	y z	1
Instruction assessors	08.45–09.05		A to F	x y z	1
Reception role-players	08.45–09.05		R1 R2 R3	a	2
IN-BASKET	08.45–09.25	3–4			TR
	08.45–10.10	5–6			TZ
DIALOGUE					
Preparation	08.45–09.05	1–3			TR
Performance	09.10–09.30	1	A and B	R1 x	1
		2	C and D	R2 y	2
		3	E and F	R3 z	3
Assessment	9.30–9.50				TR
Preparation	9.30–9.50	4–6			
Performance	9.55–10.15	4	A and E	R1 x	1
		5	B and D	R2 y	2
		6	C and F	R3 z	3
Evaluation	10.15–10.35				
MEMORANDUM					
Writing of memorandum	08.50–10.50	10–12			TR
	09.35–11.35	1–3			TR
	10.20–12.20	4–6			TR
	11.05–13.05	7–9			TR
LUNCH	11.40–12.20	1–3			R
	11.50–12.25	10–12	R1 R2 R3	a	R
	12.10–13.20		A to F	x y z	R
	12.25–13.05	4–6			R
	13.10–13.50	7–9			R
PRESENTATION					
Preparation	12.25–13.25	1–3			TR
Performance	13.30–13.50		C and F	x	1
		2	A and E	y	2
		3	B and D	z	3
Assessment	13.50–14.10				
Preparation	13.10–14.10	4–6			TR
Performance	14.15–14.35	4	B and C	x	1
		5	F and A	y	2
		6	D and E	z	3
Assessment	14.35–14.55				

1 to 12 = candidates
A to F = assessors
a, b = coordination, test room staff
x, y, z = directors

results, and at the end of the AC conducting an interview with each of the candidates.

During the AC test room managers work in the test room all day. They are responsible for handing out the assignments, taking in completed work on time, giving instructions, and making sure that candidates report to the performance rooms, where oral assignments are carried out, on time.

9.5 THE LOGISTIC PREPARATION OF AN ASSESSMENT CENTRE

Once the programme has been written, letters of invitation can be sent to candidates, assessors and role-players. Depending upon the assignment, background material might also be included in these. It is important to send the letters several days before the start of the AC. The assessors and director(s) should receive a file before or during the AC, which contains information on all the assignments and various evaluation forms. Material such as stopwatches, pens, overhead projector sheets and extra assessment material is gathered together with the help of a checklist. The candidates' material is also counted and given a number.

The AC's location deserves some attention. An AC makes use of various rooms: the test room, the performance rooms and the coordination room. Candidates are received in the test room and prepare for oral assignments and complete written assignments here. Oral assignments are carried out in performance rooms under the observation of a director and a group of assessors. The coordination room can be seen as a central reporting room. This is where AC staff are received and where the coordinator works from. Incoming phone calls for candidates and staff are also taken here.

The building in which the AC is held and the various rooms in which the assignments take place, have to meet very high standards. It is better to use rooms that are situated next door to one another and well insulated against noise. A test room on the ground floor and performance rooms on the sixth floor of a building would be far from ideal. All rooms should be at a close walking distance from one another. The size of the rooms is also important. A test room, for example, should have enough space so that tables and chairs can be arranged for examinations. The layout of performance areas depends on the assignment. The layout is much the same for the Dialogue and Presentation assignments, the only difference being the inclusion of audio-visual equipment like an overhead projector which can be used during the Presentation. It goes without saying that all rooms should be extremely quiet. Make sure that there are no alterations or removals taking place in the building, and that there are no people at work in the immediate surroundings!

Lost candidates or assessors who are wandering about trying to find performance areas can cause a lot of disturbance and unnecessary panic. A clearly marked signpost network avoids such problems. Finally, it is important that all rooms can be closed off, so that confidential information can be dealt with in private.

9.6   THE LOGISTIC CLOSE OF AN ASSESSMENT CENTRE

The results of the oral assignments are known immediately after the AC's conclusion. Written assignments still need to be evaluated at this stage. Once this is done a report is made of each candidate based on the assessment material. The report is submitted to the candidate and discussed during an interview with an adviser. Finally, the report is sent to the AC contractor with the candidate's approval. Since various people are involved in various tasks during the organisation of the AC, the actual AC sessions and its conclusion, it is advisable to keep a record of who does which activity before, and/or during, and/or after the AC.

PART 4
The Assessment Centre's Conclusion

Chapter 10

Writing Assessment Centre Reports

F.D. de Jongh

10.1 INTRODUCTION

Assessment Centre reports should be extensive. Writing an AC report is an art in itself and often very time consuming. Since most managers have a busy agenda, it is better for AC professionals to write the reports. The various aspects of writing an AC report are dealt with below.

10.2 THE FUNCTION OF AN AC REPORT

The most important function of an AC report is to give candidates adequate feedback on their performance. When candidates read the report, it should be as though a film of the AC is being played before their eyes. The report plays an essential role in the assessment interview. During this, the candidate reads the

Assessment Centres: A Practical Handbook, P. Jansen and F. de Jongh.

report and may ask questions. It is the advisor's task to find out how much the candidate recognises. Obviously, the more the candidate recognises the quicker the candidate will accept the report (see Chapter 11, Assessment Interviews). Report writers should try to be as clear as possible, making statements about demonstrated behaviour. Feedback on assignments consists of summing up demonstrated behaviour and stating the score allocated. The report may also include short texts that outline deficient areas, as well as advice about how to improve or develop certain behaviour.

The Procedure

The AC advisor who writes the reports is given candidate files. which contain instructions, observation forms, checklists and rating scales, the latter forming the basis of the report. Other material may also be used. All reports are read by a colleague–consultant and revised if necessary.

Incorporating the Rating Scales

An AC report is based almost entirely on the short texts included in the rating scales. Obviously these should be of a high quality. Assessors should be as thorough as possible when filling in rating scales – something which is emphasised during assessor training. Assessors underline texts, alter texts and often include short comments. If a relevant comment is written under the wrong category, this should be corrected by the advisor who is writing the report. Sometimes texts do not correspond with the grades; in this case it is the texts, not the grades, which may be revised. Since several assessors are used in the AC, some texts may conflict with others. In these cases the report writer can refer to his own observations if he attended the AC sessions. Although it is advisable for directors to keep a record of assessment, they should not give grades.

Conditions

In order to write an AC report the writer should be well acquainted with the practical assignments and the rating scales should be complete. The submitted material should meet a certain standard and be legible. Each consultant should try to stay

as close to the submitted texts as possible. Form, style and conclusions should not differ too much from one another. Good
training and testing by other colleagues should ensure that this
is the case. The consultant should be well acquainted with the
specific aims of the AC before writing the report; there is a great
difference between ACs used for selection and ACs used for
management development. In selection the onus is upon someone's suitability, in management development more attention is
given to development advice. It is best for report writers to act as
directors during oral assignments and to assess In-baskets and
Memorandums themselves. Furthermore, they should be well
acquainted with the dimensions that are used in the rating
scales.

10.3   WRITING REPORTS

The advisor who writes the reports should approach his work
systematically. This can be done by referring to the scheme set
out in Table 10.1.

The text included in the report should deal with one practical
assignment at a time, each assignment subdivided into dimensions which are listed in a set order. A short text, consisting of
two to four sentences, should be written under each dimension.
The text should contain as much information as possible and be
clearly written and concise. Sentences should be written in tele-
gram style (the texts included in the rating scales can be used as
an example). Obviously, there should be no spelling or gram-
matical mistakes. Particular attention should be paid to the

Table 10.1   Layout of report

Assessment centre	Confidential
Candidate	
ORAL ASSIGNMENT	
Dialogue	
Problem analysis	
Problem solving	
Interpersonal sensitivity	
Sociability	
Leadership	
Delegating and management control	
Persistence	
Decisiveness	

incongruence between grades and texts. It is very irritating to come across these types of mistakes during the assessment interview. The advisor should always keep an eye out for this and make sure that texts match their grades, *not* the other way round. Table 10.2 is an example of a report text which describes a candidate's performance during an assignment.

Summary and Conclusions

The task of writing feedback on assignments is, relatively speaking, the easiest aspect of the report. It is far more difficult to

Table 10.2 Sample report

Assessment Center	Confidential
Candidate: Mr. X	

ORAL ASSIGNMENT

Dialogue

Problem analysis
Only able to identify a limited number of problems. Did not ask enough questions. Did not pursue the underlying problems. Focused on one very obvious connection between problems.

Problem solving
Came up with a rather limited number of solutions. Having weighed up the alternatives carefully, found a good approach.

Interpersonal sensitivity
Picked up the other person's thoughts and to took them into account, to some extent. Hardly acknowledged feelings at all. Did not try to imagine how the other felt.

Sociability
Showed appreciation for the other person's qualities. Was not very tactful on the whole. Sometimes listened, sometimes did not. Let the other person finish talking, most of the time.

Leadership
Too late in stating what the interview was about. Lead the conversation in the direction he wanted it to go. Tried to stimulate the "employee" to tackle the problem.

Delegating and management control
Made the "employee" see who was responsible for solving the problem and what was expected of him. Assigned him appropriate tasks. Made clear-cut agreements. Established how and when checks would be made.

Persistence
Stuck by his decision, even though the other person tried to dissuade him.

Decisiveness
Was ready and able to hold a standpoint. Acted boldly and dared to make decisions. Did not waver.

Table 10.3 A result matrix

	Practical assignments				
	D	PR	GD	MO	IB
Dimensions					
Problem analysis	*	*	*	*	*
Problem solving	*	*	*	*	*
Interpersonal sensitivity	*	*	*		*
Sociability	*	*	*		
Leadership	*	*	*		*
Delegating and management control	*				*
Planning and organising		*		*	*
Persistence	*	*	*		
Decisiveness	*		*		

D = Dialogue   GD = Group discussion   IB = In-basket
PR = Presentation   MO = Memorandum

make a summary and draw conclusions. A systematic approach is best, this can be achieved with the help of a result matrix (see Table 10.3).

First of all, the grades should be analysed *vertically* (see Chapter 2, page 22). Then a record should made of which assignments were performed adequately and which were performed inadequately. This information should, for instance, be arranged under the categories oral assignments, Memorandum and Presentation assignments together and so forth. Secondly, the grades should be analysed *horizontally* (see Chapter 2, page 23). This is more difficult than vertical analysis. A note should be made of which dimensions had a low score, a high score or varying scores (most common). When combined, the vertical and horizontal analyses form a strength/weakness analysis. This method does allow some room for interpretation. For example:

> Mr X's performance ranged from good to below average. His performance during the In-basket was not very effective on the whole. In the other four assignments his performance ranged from good to average. In the Dialogue he did succeed in encouraging a certain readiness to change in his subordinate. The interview would have been more effective if Mr X had gone deeper into the underlying problems. His performance during the Presentation was successful. Mr X played on the spectators effectively and knew how to win them over. He stuck to his viewpoint. In the Group Discussion he put his own department's interests first, but showed willingness to tackle the problem together with the rest. His Memorandum was systematic and well structured. It was legible enough. The consideration of the *fors* and *against*s did not lead automatically to the chosen alternative. Mr X's approach to the In-basket was rather disorganised. He did not delegate enough. The solutions were

badly worked out. If we take a look at the management dimensions specifically, then we see that *Problem solving*, *Leadership*, *Persistence*, and *Decisiveness* were assessed as average to good in all assignments. His performance in the remaining dimensions was inconsistent; assessments of average and good are interchanged with those of below average and poor.

Conclusion and Recommendations

During a selection AC the summary is followed by a conclusion. This might be phrased as follows: "This candidate has shown (in)sufficient evidence of having the required management qualities", or in the case of varying scores: "This candidate was not able to use his capacities to equal effect in all the assignments." This is followed by a list of development points, either on assignment level (vertically) or dimension level (horizontally) or combinations of both. For example:

'Based on the behaviour that Mr X demonstrated during this Assessment Centre, we conclude that the following areas require extra attention and development:

- The ability to employ various management qualities effectively in various situations.
- The ability to investigate a problem's underlying causes by asking further questions.
- The ability to reach agreements that satisfy both parties.
- The awareness of the need for delegating tasks and responsibilities.'

10.4 MANAGEMENT DEVELOPMENT RECOMMENDATIONS

On the basis of an AC report, it is fairly simple to indicate which areas need development. It is, however, far more difficult to draw up recommendations for management-development. In order to make a soundly based MD recommendation, one should find out extra information about the candidate. First, what type of ambitions does the candidate have? Obviously, if candidates do not have any specific ambitions, there is no need to go any further. Secondly, is the candidate willing to learn? After this it should be fairly clear how well the candidate accepts the development areas and is ready to learn. Other information needed will include: the candidate's mobility (age plays an important role in this); preference for certain learning methods, or a favourite learning environment (individual, learning based on experience, with or without a coach, learning on the job, project leadership, interim work, training and courses); learning style, personality, intelligence, values, and norms. Most of this information can be obtained during an interview and, if necessary, supplemented with test material.

Once this information has been established and the relevant points extracted, a management development recommendation can be written. There follows a discussion with the AC contractor to decide how these recommendations should be implemented.

Training to Write Reports

An AC report is very different from a psychological report. An AC report looks at several separate assignments, which is hardly ever the case in psychological reports. An AC report also records demonstrated behaviour. Finally, in a psychological report, unlike in AC reports, test data is interpreted in a psychological way. Many psychologists regard this as an essential part of their work. Summaries and conclusions of AC reports are easy to trace back and in this way final conclusions are more accessible to the layman. It is quite a task for professional psychologists to learn how to write an AC report, since they are not allowed to do what they are good at, ie interpretation, but required to do what they are *not* used to, ie provide concrete feedback on concrete behaviour. A training course in AC reporting is often the best option. The training course deals with the aspects mentioned in this chapter. Trainees work in groups of two which are frequently interchanged. They practice writing texts about various assignments, based on the same assessment material. These texts are compared for similarities, differences and use of language. Extra attention is given to writing summaries and conclusions.

Chapter 11

Assessment Interviews

F.D. de Jongh

11.1 INTRODUCTION

An assessment interview is an essential part of an AC. Candidates have a right to feedback on their performance. The previous chapter concentrated on the written feedback they receive in the form of a report. The focus of this chapter is the verbal feedback used during an assessment interview. Before the assessment interview takes place it is important to determine the interview's objectives. The consultant responsible for conducting the interview should know how an AC is constructed, be able to command various conversation and intervention techniques and, more importantly, have the necessary personal qualities.

11.2 OBJECTIVES

The objective of an assessment interview depends on the line of approach that the advisor takes. Both the advisor and the contractor, as well as the candidate, may have particular intentions.

Assessment Centres: A Practical Handbook, P. Jansen and F. de Jongh.
© 1997 John Wiley & Sons Ltd.

On the other hand, the interview may have predetermined objectives.

General Objectives

An assessment interview should consist of structured feedback based on the observation and assessment of a candidate's behaviour during assignments. The various conclusions based on this behaviour are dealt with and then the candidate is given advice.

The Advisor's Objectives

The advisor may have one or more of the following objectives:

- to inform candidates about the observation and assessment of their behaviour during the AC;
- to clarify the report;
- to stimulate recognition of what happened during the AC;
- to help candidates accept the report;
- to motivate candidates to work on their weaknesses.

The Candidate's Objectives

The candidate's objectives are not known until the interview takes place. It is the advisor's task to find out what these are, using a direct or indirect line of approach.

Possible objectives may include:

- clarification, or proof of the contrary;
- acknowledgement or understanding of the contrary (in this case the candidate may say, for example, "You must understand that this sounds totally unfamiliar?");
- acceptance understanding of the contrary;
- motivation or understanding of the contrary;
- criticism of the report and/or appreciation of it.
- obstruction of the report;
- amendment of a decision;
- report the consequences and show understanding for this;
- expression of feelings.

Obviously, the course of an assessment interview is strongly influenced by the candidate's intentions. In the case of resistance or communication problems, the consultant should always determine whether this is due to ambiguous or conflicting objectives.

The Contractor's Objectives

The contractor uses the AC to achieve a specific aim. This is also the case with the assessment interview. If the AC is designed for selection, the contractor expects candidates to be informed about their performance. If the AC was intended for management development, the advisor should discuss the candidate's performance as well as development potential. The contractor may also expect the advisor to soften the blow in the event of bad news. If a candidate's expectations were high and yet the results were disappointing, the consultant would have to invest more time in helping the candidate to deal with this fact. Sometimes, a second interview may be necessary.

11.3 WHAT THE ADVISOR SHOULD KNOW

The consultant should know whether the AC is used for the purposes of selection or management development, be familiar with the AC assignments and have the dimensions and rating scales ready. The consultant should know how the AC progressed and how the candidate evaluated it. It is a good idea for the advisor to work as a director during the AC, to have assessed the written assignments and written the report, or at least be familiar with its content. The consultant should also know if there were any unusual occurrences during the AC. Finally, the advisor should have a global idea of what the contractor can offer the candidate in terms of training and work experience.

11.4 INTERVIEW TECHNIQUES

An advisor should be able to deal with various interview techniques. The most important are the appraisal technique, the feedback technique and the advisory technique. It is also essential to know what type of techniques are required when relating "bad news".

The Appraisal Technique

The appraisal technique consists of informing a candidate of his assessment. This can be done in a "Tell/sell" way or in a "Tell/listen" way. With the "Tell/sell" approach the report is, if you like, sold to the candidate. The consultant speaks and the candidate listens. If the consultant adopts this approach it is important that the consultant can support his arguments with supplementary information. A "Tell/sell" approach can take on the character of a "Yes, but" discussion, on both sides. With the "Tell/listen" approach the candidate talks more than the consultant. The consultant says what he has to say and then spends most of the time listening. Sometimes candidates find this approach rather vague and unsettling, because the consultant is very understanding about the candidate's resistance on the one hand, yet refuses to alter his standpoint. During an assessment interview it is useful to have some practice at breaking bad news. Timing is essential. The consultant should try to find the right way and the right moment to deal the blow, and then help the candidate to accept this.

The Feedback Technique

The feedback technique aims to supply candidates with information about behaviour that they were unaware of, or only partially aware of but that was apparent to others during the AC.
   Feedback should be:

- descriptive
- specific
- in the candidate's interests
- useful
- desired
- given at the right moment
- clearly and precisely formulated
- correct.

Giving and receiving feedback is a communicative and relational process. It is a rather complicated form of communication, and should be based on the following.

Conditions for Giving Feedback

In order to give feedback, the consultant should:

- be able to give feedback in the way that has been previously described;
- be social minded.
- be open to additional information;
- be able to refrain from moralising and subjective interpretations;
- not confuse feedback with value judgements;
- not be over-insistent with information;
- be open and honest;
- admit that they can also make mistakes.

It is obvious that the feedback interview will run more smoothly if the consultant is able to meet certain requirements. Since the advisory relationship between the candidate and the advisor is short-lived, the advisor may enter into an interview where the candidate fails to fulfil all sorts of conditions. It would be wonderful if the candidate was motivated to receive feedback and was open to the impressions that others had formed. The realisation of these conditions should be discussed during the intake procedure. Candidates who reject feedback or feel no need to work on their own development should be advised not to take part.

The Advisory Technique

The advisory technique consists of suggesting ways in which candidates can improve their weaknesses. This should only be carried out if candidates have acknowledged these weaknesses and are motivated to improve them. The "Tell/listen" method is the most appropriate approach in this interview.

11.5 INTERVENTIONS

The various forms of techniques that we have mentioned share some similarities and some differences. These are related to the type of actions that are necessary to conduct the interview in the right way, namely, choosing the appropriate action at the right moment. Such actions are called "interventions". The most important interventions are listed below:

- active listening
- summarising
- reflecting thoughts and feelings
- structuring
- asking further questions
- supporting
- adding information by questioning
- interpreting
- informing
- suggesting and advising
- judging.

Advisors should have a good command of all interventions and be able to determine which ones are appropriate to which form of interview. This is illustrated in Table 11.1. Interventions have been divided into possible and necessary interventions and into two frames of reference; that of the candidate and that of the advisor.

If we compare the different techniques, it would seem that interventions play an important role in all techniques, from the candidate's point of view. In the feedback techniques they are necessary, even. An advisor should be able to work with these interventions and know which one to use at which moment. For junior advisors this is a matter of trial and error. If the candidate becomes defensive, or clams up, it is likely that the advisor has either forgotten to use an intervention or has used the wrong one. Many inappropriate interventions stem from the consultants. In other words, the consultants may be more occupied with his own thoughts and feelings than those of the candidate. If the right interventions are used in the right situations, the candidate will be encouraged to reveal more. To summarise, consultants should be well aware of what type of interview they are conducting and what types of interventions should be placed at which moments.

11.6   STRUCTURING THE INTERVIEW

The AC assessment interview should be structured systematically. Approximately one hour is reserved for the interview. The advisor should have read and preferably written the report. He should have looked at the candidate's file and examined the evaluation form. An assessment interview is conducted

Table 11.1 Interventions in assessment interviews

Interventions in assessment interviews	Feedback techniques	Appraisal techniques	Advisory techniques
CANDIDATE'S FRAME OF REFERENCE			
Active listening Eye contact, nodding, "hhm" repeating a word.	○	○	○
Summarising Briefly say what you heard the other person say, preferably in your own words, in this way find out if you understood it properly.	○	□	□
Reflecting thoughts and feelings Indicate what you thought the other person felt or thought implicitly or explicitly.	○	○	□
Structuring Bring structure into a long conversation, pointing towards connections, or possible contradictions.	○	□	□
Asking further questions Pursue what the other person said; for your own clarification, or to help the other person to explore the area in more detail or to make things concrete.	○	□	□
Supporting Acknowledge what has happened; for example, wrong, but not fatal, difficult, but not impossible; confirm.	○	○	□
ADVISOR'S FRAME OF REFERENCE			
Adding information by asking questions Ask questions from your own point of view, say what might not have been discussed.		□	○
Interpreting Repeat what the other person said, linking this to what you see as a possible explanation.		○	□
Informing Relate something based on your own knowledge or experience in answer to a question or, on your own initiative.	○	□	○
Suggesting Indicate where the solution might be found.		□	○
Advising Emphasise which direction you think is most preferable or accessible to the other person.		□	○
Judging Indicate what, according to you, was right, not right, effective, ineffective, about the candidate's performance during the AC.		○	○

○ = Necessary intervention
□ = Possible intervention

in various stages, for example: the interview proposition, assessment, feedback, advice, and agreements.

Stage 1: Interview Proposition

The consultant suggests what the conversation could focus on and asks whether the candidate agrees with this, for example:

- read the report
- explain the text
- candidate's objectives
- feedback
- advice
- agreements.

Stage 2: Appraisal

At this stage of the interview the report should be read and any ambiguities clarified. The advisor might explain why certain conclusions have been made. A reflection on feeling would be appropriate at this stage. Prior knowledge of the evaluation form would also be useful. The consultant could refer to this to see if the results are disappointing or otherwise.

The Candidate's Objectives

After reading the report, the candidate often formulates or begins to formulate an objective for the interview. It is the consultant's task to make his objectives and that of the candidate explicit and to determine, together with the candidate, what the interview's objective should be. The consultant should be on the lookout for the negative consequences of the AC for the candidate. Sometimes this can be the only reason why the candidate refuses to accept the outcome.

Stage 3: Feedback

Stage 2 can lead very gradually to Stage 3. But feedback is more than explaining the text. When giving feedback the consultant should help the candidate to relive the AC. Sometimes the consultant can ask what the candidate has seen or read. Sometimes this should take place with the candidate's help. There may only be full acknowledgement when the candidate found the AC report clear and accepted the feedback.

Stage 4: Advising

If both the consultant and the candidate feels that the candidate's performance corresponds with the candidate's capabilities, then advice can be given. This will be based on any revealed weaknesses in dimensions or assignments, and should consider what help can be offered in the way of coaching, courses and further training. The consultant should know what the contractor is able to offer in respect to this.

Stage 5: Agreements

At the end of the interview agreements should be made. First, the consultant should ask the candidate's permission to send the report to the contractor. Then plans for further development can be discussed. This can not be discussed at any length during the AC assessment interview. To make a plan for further development, points for consideration are: ambition, willingness to learn, mobility, learning style and personality. The AC does not provide this type of information, it should be gathered elsewhere, and only with the contractor's permission. Once agreements have been made it is time to round off the interview with an evaluative question or comment, if required.

11.7   PERSONAL QUALITIES

Apart from having all types of skills, a consultant should possess certain personal qualities. Disappointed candidates will most certainly try to reduce or transfer their responsibility. The assignments' validity might be put into question, or the time that was assigned for preparation. A candidate may criticise the length of the AC, or the influence of role-players or assessors, or mention possible disruptions. A consultant should be able to listen to this type of criticism without immediately becoming defensive. The consultant might explain why the AC was conducted in this way, if the candidate seems open to explanations. Obviously, one cannot go into too much detail about methodology. The candidate's response also depends on the consultant's air of authority. In order to advise managers on their future development, consultants should be convinced that they have something to offer. If not, even though their advice is good and accurate, they will not be given much credit for it.

_____ Chapter 12

Aftercare

C.H. Reijerse

12.1   INTRODUCTION

At the end of an Assessment Centre some candidates may need
guidance and support. This is referred to as aftercare. There is
no set formula for providing aftercare. In order to determine the
most appropriate form of aftercare, one should think carefully
about the aims and consequences of each Assessment Centre.
Obviously, the use of ACs for the purposes of measuring potential and performance should have its own place in the larger
framework of Human Resource Management within an organisation. This chapter focuses upon the following themes in relation to aftercare:

a. The setting in which the AC takes place.
b. How to take the AC's outcomes further.
c. How to deal with disappointed candidates and the role that
    counselling plays in this.
d. The use of AC methodology for malfunctioning managers.

Assessment Centres: A Practical Handbook, P. Jansen and F. de Jongh.
© 1997 John Wiley & Sons Ltd.

12.2   THE SETTING

The type of aftercare that candidates receive depends on the aims of the AC they participated in. There are two main types of Assessment Centres:

1. Those used for selection procedures.
2. Those used for career guidance and management development procedures (see also Chapter 15).

Selection Procedures

These can be divided into two categories: external and internal procedures. External candidates have no relationship with the company, therefore, aftercare can be restricted to feedback in an assessment interview (see Chapter 11). Aftercare is far more important in the case of internal procedures. The best way to prevent rejected employees from feeling discouraged, angry or despondent is to provide a follow-up to the assessment interview.

Career Guidance and Management Development Programmes

In the case of internal career or MD training programmes, aftercare is essential. In these cases, the measurement of performance and potential is only one part of a series of activities that are geared towards achieving a certain aim, ie improving someone's chances of being promoted to a key function. In the job market, external candidates are often not directly available for top management or specialised jobs. During the past years several organisations have started career guidance programmes for jobs lower down in the scale. More and more organisations recognise the need to increase the workforce's mobility, so that the various processes involved in someone's transition from one job to another can be better planned and directed.

12.3   FOLLOW-UP ACTIVITIES

What is the purpose of follow-up activities?

Activities that are geared towards the individual:

education
training
coaching/supervision
counselling.

Organisations have the following at their disposal:

job rotation/interim tasks
registration of interest
temporary assignments
mentoring
providing information about current and near-future vacancies.

The main aim of ACs is to help organisations find the right person for the job.

Example 1   Management potential development programme

A computer company uses internal candidates for its management vacancies. Once every two years, the company has to find out what type of management potential is available internally. Suitable employees are selected and then participate in a training and guidance programme. The procedure is carried out as follows:

- Employees interested in a management job are asked to submit themselves for a MD programme.
- Screening of candidates by means of an interview (motivation).
- AC geared towards management skills.
- Suitable candidates move on to management positions.
- Employees who lack the necessary skills follow a supplementary training programme. This consists of the following steps:

    Step 1: Training general management skills, including assessment
    Step 2: Acquaintance with various jobs within the company.
    Step 3: Temporary assignments based on the tasks that the actual job would entail are carried out under the guidance of a mentor:
    – on the job training
    – assessment
    – transition to the desired job in phases.

Assessors should be involved in AC aftercare as much as possible. In this way maximum use can be made of the trust that has been built up during the AC.

Secondly, in the context of career guidance, employees may take part in an AC on their own initiative, to get a better idea of their strengths and weaknesses.

Example 2 Women in focus

A programme was carried out by an advice bureau which specialised in the area of ACs and MD. The programme aimed at increasing the number of women in management functions and was known as "Women in focus". The target group consisted of women from higher educational backgrounds in non-managerial positions. Participants could sign up for the programme on their own initiative. The programme consisted of the following:

Step 1: Intake interview.

Step 2: Workshop in career orientation, geared towards discovering strengths/ weaknesses and career goals.

Step 3: AC assessment of various skills by assessors.

Step 4: Follow-up day during which the results of steps 2 and 3 are integrated. Information session given by women with managerial positions in a government ministry.

Step 5: At the participant's request, an interview with a personnel consultant about her future prospects.

For the best results, personnel development activities should be geared towards the strategic needs of the organisation and the individual career goals of employees. The balance may sway to one side, but the guiding factor should always be the improvement of the workforce's mobility, in the interests of company and individual.

Table 12.1 indicates when aftercare should be provided, in relation to the aims of the AC and the setting in which it takes place.

12.4 IMPLEMENTATION OF SELECTION AND MANAGEMENT DEVELOPMENT RESULTS

The AC's outcome usually points towards a few areas that candidates need to improve on. Depending on the dimensions

Table 12.1 Setting and aftercare activities

Setting	Assessment interview	Follow-up activities (aftercare)
External selection	Facultative	No
Internal selection	Yes	Yes, especially in the interests of the individual
Assessment of potential geared towards the organisation	Yes	Yes, in the interests of the organisation and the individual
Assessment of potential geared towards the individual	Yes	Sometimes, especially in the interests of the individual

involved, the experience, the age and the candidate's approach to learning, the methods of improvement will be chosen on the basis of know-how, personal attitudes and skills. Areas like "Problem analysis" and, to a lesser extent, "Planning and Organising" and "Creativity" are related to someone's intellectual and learning capacities. Professional educational programmes and training courses are used in cases where improvement is possible. Courses in time management teach ways in which to plan and organise work more efficiently. Intuitive and creative thinking can be improved by practising new ways of approaching problems. There are numerous courses and workshops available in these areas.

"Interpersonal sensitivity", "Sociability", "Leadership", and "Delegating and management control" fall under the category of social skills. Training courses in management skills and personal effectiveness can be used to improve these areas. The courses are designed so that participants can try out different types of behaviour in relatively safe environments, and register the effect this has on others. Sometimes problems are caused by candidates being unaware of the sources of their behaviour and reactions. In these cases, more intensive and personal guidance methods would be appropriate, such as counselling.

Example 3 The irritated personnel manager

A personnel manager was confused about why he was always so irritated whenever his manager asked him questions about work. He never seemed to get irritated by questions from colleagues. His manager was rather condescending, but that was not the problem. The personnel officer talked about this with others and tried to examine the problem in more detail. In doing so he realised that the manager made him feel inadequate and insecure. He always tried to avoid further questions by keeping his answers short and becoming more and more irritated in the process. The manager was unsettled by this and frequently checked up on the personnel manager.

The personnel manager will not be able to change this situation until he gains more insight into the sources of his thoughts and feelings.

Qualities like initiative, tenacity, persistence and decisiveness are not easy to improve. Different levels of self confidence and temperament in individuals are manifested in their inclination to action. Self confidence can be increased by further learning, in the form of professional and technical training courses, for example. If someone's weaknesses are related to personal blocks and can not be improved by acquiring extra skills and knowledge, a more intensive form of guidance is necessary. Coaching, counselling, mentoring and supervision offer excellent opportunities for providing guidance in learning areas. In conversation with a counsellor or advisor, employees are taught to deal with difficult situations more effectively.

During these conversations problem situations are closely analysed. Inadequate reactions are examined. Then alternatives are put forward for the employee to try out. This method is also used during mentoring and coaching. The emphasis is on the immediate improvement of concrete behaviour manifested in work situations. In counselling and often in supervision, the onus is upon more personal aspects.

12.5   DEALING WITH DISAPPOINTED CANDIDATES, AND COUNSELLING

In an assessment interview it is important to deal with disappointed candidates carefully, especially in the case of internal selection procedures which provide little or no follow-up activities. Candidates with poor results worry, quite justifiably, about what type of effect this will have on their position in the organisation. "What do the assessors do with the information?"; "Will people start to doubt whether I am suitable for the job I do now?" are some of the questions that they might ask. Providing reassurance and promising to keep the AC results confidential is all that one can do in this type of situation. But will assessors, especially internal assessors, really forget this type of incident or be able to hold back information on the candidate in the future? On the one hand a high degree of integrity is required of assessors. On the other hand, it is not always possible or desirable to isolate information from ACs. The Personnel Department or the person in charge of MD, is responsible for dealing with this type of information and the consequences that it might involve. It is far better for the employee and the organisation to talk openly about poor AC results, and any doubts that may have been raised about the employee's job performance.

Counselling

Candidates may complain that the AC results are inaccurate. If their performance of a Presentation, for example, was assessed as poor, they may reply by claiming that the presentations that they did in the past were always well received. Candidates will only accept and gain insight into their strengths and weaknesses if the AC results are integrated into the image that they have of themselves. An AC will not be effective unless candidates achieve a deeper self awareness. When they have reached this stage, support can be offered in the work environment, by colleagues and superiors. Participants who cannot combine the AC results with the idea that they have formed of themselves, need guidance. The aim of counselling is to increase the candidates' acceptance of the AC's results and adapt the way in which candidates view their abilities. Counselling should be offered if the assessment interview did not offer enough solace and if the AC was used for career guidance or management development. Counselling should deal with the following:

- What type of self-image does the candidate have?
- According to the candidate, how do other people view him, at work and in his personal life, and why?
- How do these two conclusions relate to one another and how do they differ from each other?
- How does this relate to the AC results?

Our self-image is formed at an early age, and is influenced by the way in which the environment reacts to our behaviour. A candidate's work situation and the AC assessors can shed some light on this. If the assessors are internal, there should not be too much disparity between the two. On the other hand, we should avoid jumping to conclusions. A candidate with low AC results may claim to receive positive feedback from managers at work. In this case, one should not immediately assume that the candidate has a distorted view of things. Different people do, of course, judge people differently. Furthermore, desirable behaviour is situation dependent.

Example 4 Back to before

An employee worked as a manager on a temporary project for two years. When the job was finished, he took part in a career guidance programme and was assessed on management skills in an AC. The results were not very promising and revealed that he was not suitable for a management position. He had low scores in the areas "Planning and Organising" and "Decisiveness". During the assessment interview, he mentioned that he had worked as a manager for a while. He admitted, quite reluctantly, that this had not gone very smoothly, but said that his colleagues were to blame. He was keen to work as a manager again and prove that he was capable of the job. He was willing to consult a career advisor or psychologist to find out what the best course of action would be. There followed a series of 20 conversations, spread over eight months. During these sessions he discussed what he thought about himself and the difference between what he wanted to be and what he was. He also talked about his family background. His parents had very high expectations of him and he always felt the need to distinguish himself from his brothers and sisters. During counselling he realised that this was why he felt so driven to master his weaknesses and prove that he could be a manager. He found out that he felt much better when working in a supportive role. He worked more effectively and felt more relaxed because he did not have to carry the end responsibility. He liked to have clearly defined responsibilities. During counselling, he was offered another job within his own firm; one that he was perfectly suited to. He became the secretary of a project group that dealt with the implementation of mid-term policies in his field. Three months later, he had settled into his job and received high praise for his work from his manager and colleagues.

12.6   MALFUNCTIONING MANAGERS

'Is there any point in letting malfunctioning managers take part in an AC?' is a question that assessment consultants are often asked. Organisations often assume that the AC will solve this by confronting the manager with his shortcomings and making the manager realise that he is not doing his job properly. Poor performance, however, is often due to someone feeling powerless or at an *impasse*. If the AC is used as a veiled evaluation or exam, companies might be confronted with a far more positive result than they had expected. A deadlock situation between employer and employee demands accurate problem analysis involving both parties. When this has been carried out an AC might provide a solution to the problem. The organisation should confer with the employee in question and have a clear idea of what type of follow-up activities should be used.

PART 5

Evaluation of the
Assessment Centre

Chapter 13

The Evaluation of Assessment Centres

F.D. de Jongh

13.1 INTRODUCTION

What are the main criteria for a successful Assessment Centre? Candidates and assessors should find the assignments valid, and the AC personnel (the directors, role-players, logistic manager and test room staff) should create an environment that candidates trust and feel at ease in. Contractors will feel that an AC was successful if they were able to put the information it supplied to good use. We can find out if an AC fulfilled this criteria by asking all those who took part to give their opinion. This can be done during a short conversation, or by means of a questionnaire.

13.2 CONTRACTORS

Organisations use ACs for selection, management development or outplacement. The contracting organisation should always be

Assessment Centres: A Practical Handbook, P. Jansen and F. de Jongh.
© 1997 John Wiley & Sons Ltd.

asked if they found the AC results useful. This might be done after the AC results have been disclosed, or during a phone call if the AC reports were sent by post. If the AC was used for selection purposes, the results are presented in such a way that the contractor can compare these with other sources of information on the candidate (Curriculum Vitae and references) to arrive at a decision. In the event of management development or outplacement, follow-up activities are carried out, which may or may not involve an AC advisor.

If the contractor is dissatisfied with the quality of the AC results, then it is important to find out if this is due to a specific situation or to the AC as a whole. In both cases, one should find out how to make the contractor happier. One should find out which area the criticism is restricted to: the information that was given beforehand, the actual AC, the report, the assessment interviews, or what? If several contractors criticise one or more areas, then improvements should be made.

13.3   OTHER PARTICIPANTS

Every AC is evaluated and this involves everyone who participated in it:

- candidates
- role-players
- assessors
- directors
- logistic manager
- test room staff.

A questionnaire is used for this purpose. First, several general questions are asked concerning, for example:

- the material that was sent to people at home
- treatment during the AC
- accommodation
- the programme, was it clear, well-organised?
- candidate guidance.

Then each assignment is evaluated separately. The same questions are asked about each assignment and are based on the following:

- clarity
- how difficult
- closeness to reality
- relevance
- conducive to showing abilities
- preparation time
- performance time
- quality of instructions.

Figure 13.1 shows a section of an evaluation questionnaire based on the Dialogue assignment. Once all the evaluative information has been gathered, one can decide if the criticism is incidental or structural. In the event of incidental criticism one should come up with *ad hoc* solutions. Structural improvements will have to be made in the case of fundamental criticism.

13.4 AFTERSALES

The contractor and the participants are asked to give an evaluation of the AC immediately after receiving the results. This can be referred to as evaluation on immediate reaction level. Later

```
┌─────────────────────────────────────────────────────────────┐
│  3.  Dialogue                                                 │
│      ─────────────────                                        │
│  a.  I found the dialogue                                     │
│      assessment:                                              │
│                          1   2   3   4   5   6   7            │
│              confusing   □   □   □   □   □   □   □  clear      │
│               difficult  □   □   □   □   □   □   □  easy       │
│             unrealistic  □   □   □   □   □   □   □  realistic  │
│              irrelevant  □   □   □   □   □   □   □  relevant   │
│         not conducive to □   □   □   □   □   □   □  conducive to│
│       showing my abilities                           showing my abilities│
│                                                               │
│  b.  During the interview I had:                              │
│                          1   2   3   4   5   6   7            │
│             insufficient □   □   □   □   □   □   □  sufficient │
│          preparation time                          preparation time│
│             insufficient □   □   □   □   □   □   □  sufficient │
│              instruction                           instruction │
│             insufficient □   □   □   □   □   □   □  sufficient │
│          performance time                          performance time│
└─────────────────────────────────────────────────────────────┘
```

Figure 13.1 Section of the evaluation questionnaire for the dialogue assignment

on, however, some people may wonder if the AC had been worthwhile. It is important to provide an opportunity for people to discuss this, either formally or informally. If the predictive value of an AC is put into doubt, an investigation should be made into the validity of the AC's predictions (See Chapter 14). Less formally, one might contact the contracting organisation and ask how useful the AC has been.

The Value of Assessment Centres

P. van der Maesen de Sombreff and J. de Veer

14.1 INTRODUCTION

More and more companies are becoming interested in ACs, but
what makes them so appealing? This has a lot to do with the
way in which the assignments are designed; they are very true
to life and involve practical, relevant tasks that elicit concrete
behaviour. This type of criteria encourages acceptance from AC
contractors and participants. For a professional evaluation of the
AC method, however, we cannot rely on face values but require
proof that the ACs results are accurate. This can be achieved by
empirical investigation, based on the following questions:

- How accurate are the predictions of future performance?
- In what way can ACs be seen as a supplement to other
  methods of predicting future performance?

The financial returns of an AC is another crucial aspect of its
validity. Are organisations that use ACs more profitable than

Assessment Centres: A Practical Handbook, P. Jansen and F. de Jongh.

those who do not? Since companies invest large amounts of money in ACs it is quite natural for them to be interested in cost-benefit analyses. When we determine the financial returns of an AC we should not only focus on the criterion of finding the right person for the job, but also consider the effects that the new employee will have on the quality of other activities that contribute to the organisation's financial returns.

14.2 HOW TO INVESTIGATE WHETHER AN AC IS PREDICTIVE

Predictors and Criteria

When people are assessed in an AC, they are given several scores which indicate how well they performed in the AC assignments or assessment dimensions. At the end of the AC these scores are combined to make a final score which denotes the candidate's global effectiveness or potential. This score is referred to as the *predictor*. A candidate's success in a job or career is the subject of prediction, otherwise known as the *criterion*. Which factors determine the criterion?

- effectiveness in a managerial function
- rate of promotion
- management potential
- salary growth.

Validity

To find out if the predictors predicted the criteria accurately, we examine the scores per predictor and criterion of a large group of AC participants, and determine the correlation between the two scores. The correlation is known as *the predictive validity*. It can range from minus one to one. A validity of one is perfect and indicates that a candidate's rank in the criterion hierarchy corresponds exactly with their place on the predictor scale. A validity of nought means that there is no relationship between predictor and criterion, in other words, the same result could have been achieved by drawing lots. A negative validity indicates that someone scored high on the predictor and low on the criterion or vice versa. This would be shown in the case of a less successful manager typifying top management behaviour, for example. The closer to one the better the validity. A score of one is, however, impossible. This can be due to several reasons:

- Someone's success at work is due not only to their own efforts but also to support from managers and colleagues.
- Neither the predictor nor the criterion are perfect measures. They are unreliable to a certain extent.
- It is unlikely that the predictor will cover all areas of the criterion. We are dealing with human behaviour after all.
- Organisations sometimes base selection decisions on the predictor's outcome. Candidates with a high score on the predictor have a higher chance of being employed or promoted.

Rejected candidates cannot be included in the correlation because they do not supply criterion information. This decreases the validity. One should also be aware of factors that artificially increase the validity, for example, assessors who are engaged in the assessment of someone's performance in their job (criterion), who may be influenced by this person's result in the AC (predictor).

Research into the Validity of ACs

AC methods have been in use since the beginning of this century and research has been carried out on their validity ever since. The results were quite satisfactory, the validity significant often scored higher than nought. It would seem that potential is easier to predict than actual job performance. The results of research carried out before 1977 came up with validities of 0.63 for the prediction of potential, and 0.33 for the prediction of job performance. These findings raised some questions (cf Klimoski and Brickner) about how objective assessors are. How far are they influenced by a candidate's ability to conform with the values and norms of future employees? Being liked by one's boss seemed to be a better indication of someone's chances of promotion than their achievement at work. If this was true, then the use of ACs would perpetuate bad practices, ie the selection of sitting manager clones. On the other hand, a candidate's ability to fit in with an existing team is an important predictor of his/her ability to cooperate.

Meta-analysis

Research in the area of AC validity produced differing results. This was probably due to the great differences in the size of the separate surveys. The target groups ranged from 12 to several thousand AC participants (research carried out by Moses and his team for AT&T).

It is very difficult to make general statements about the validity of ACs, based on surveys that differ so greatly in terms of criterion data and size. During the past 15 years, psychologists have developed a new methodology which can be applied to investigations into validity. This methodology is known as "meta-analysis" and can be used to combine the results from various studies. Meta-analysis is certainly not 100% reliable, because it involves subjective decisions; in the classification of the various studies, for example. The largest meta-analysis of ACs was carried out in 1987 by Gaugler, Rosenthal, Thornton and Bentson.

14.3   THE RESEARCH OF GAUGLER *ET AL.* (1987)

Research Data

The research looked at 50 AC validity surveys which reported on 107 validities. These surveys were based on 12,000 people who were assessed in an AC. Most of the surveys date from between 1975 and 1985.

The Method

Gaugler and his colleagues were interested in the real validity of the AC based on various criteria details. We should not put too much faith in the results of one validity study; this depends on the size of the survey. Obviously, the larger the survey the more representative the results. When combining the results of various studies, the validities based on large target groups have more weight than validities based on smaller target groups. The extent to which predictors are used in selection, is also taken into account, when the separate validity studies are combined. The main purpose of meta-analysis is to determine whether the validity of ACs is systematically higher than nought. An affirmative answer confirms that the AC is valid.

Another matter that Gaugler and his team wanted to explain was the variation in validities. How would this be reduced if one subtracted all the "misleading" factors like differences in survey size, for example? If the differences still remain, companies would be well advised to adopt a critical approach when choosing an AC. After all, there are differences in quality. A third aim of Gaugler's research was to look at the factors that undermine an AC's predictive value. For practical reasons, it is very important for AC developers and users to know which factors influence the AC's validity.

Results

The true validity of all the surveys when combined was 0.37. This is lower than the validity of the intelligence test, which was around 0.5, but higher than the most common method, the unstructured interview, which resulted in a validity of 0.25. The answer to the first question, whether the AC is a valid instrument, turned out to be positive: 90% of the ACs had a validity of 0.21 or more. The degree of validity appeared to be dependent upon the nature of the criterion: the validity was 0.36 if the criterion consisted of assessment of performance, and 0.53 if the criterion was the evaluation of potential. The question posed by Klimoski and Brickner is still valid. Although the AC method is reliable, the differences in validity still remain. ACs are never exactly the same, which will also lead to differences in financial returns.

Gaugler and his team researched the factors that influenced the validity of ACs. In many cases, the studies that were used in the meta-analysis did not give information on the exact circumstances of the AC's construction, for example, the number of hours that were assigned to assessor training, the assimilation of information etc. This meant that Gaugler could not use all the surveys. In this way the results in this area were not as definitive as they could have been. Further research is needed.

The following trends can be traced from Gaugler's material:

- ACs work better when a large number of different assignments are used.
- ACs in which peers assess one another's performance are better than those assessed by managers. (But would an AC without managers have adverse effects on the organisation, and lead to it neglecting its responsibility for assessment?)

- ACs that evaluate on dimensions have a lower validity than ACs which evaluate performance in assignments (this is denoted as "situational assessment", see Chapter 2).

Gaugler's results pointed towards the need for research in the following areas:

- At which point does assessor training result in a decrease in the returns?
- This question should also be applied to:
  - the number of assessors in relationship to the number of candidates; and
  - the number of hours that the assessors use to consult one another to arrive at a final assessment result.

14.4 THE COSTS OF AN ASSESSMENT CENTRE

The saying "Nothing ventured nothing gained" is pertinent to the business world. All investments involve certain risks. However, most organisations that consider using an AC put a great deal of emphasis on the costs and financial returns that it might entail. The various participants: the advisors, the contractor, the candidates (internal / external), the role-players/ actors, the administrative and organisational support, obviously incur certain costs. The most important cost categories are dealt with below.

Development Costs

A great deal of time and effort is put into the development of ACs. Sometimes the AC is made to measure and developed by an organisation internally or by an advice bureau. Sometimes ACs are put together using the standard components that the advice bureau has in stock. In this case one would pay for the development costs indirectly via the acquisition price. Organisations can write off the development costs over the number of participants and over the number of years that the AC is used. The write-off term plays an important role in whether companies opt for ACs that are made to measure or ready made. ACs will have to be revised or updated from time to time if, for example, the target job is altered, or if participants are too familiar with the assignments.

Development costs can be subdivided as follows:

- *The costs involved in employing advisors*
  Costs that are involved in job analysis (for example, during critical incident interviews), the development of assignments, the development of score instructions, writing instruction booklets, drawing up a plan. Trail runs and consultations between contractor and advisors also involve costs. The development of the AC programme and the development of training courses for assessors and role-players also fall under this category.
- *The contractor's costs*
  The contractor invests time in consultations with the advisor, in critical incident interviews and trial runs.
- *Administrative support costs*
  In the event of external advisors the costs will be directly expressed in declarations. As for the costs of internal staff there are three standpoints and all of them lead to very different results.
  - Standpoint 1 ("no cost"): The assessment and development of (future) staff is an essential task within an organisation. This task is an integral part of management work. Therefore, managers should not ask for extra pay for their work in an AC.
  - Standpoint 2 ("cost price", recommended by the authors): The assessment and development of (future) employees can be carried out using various methods that involve both candidates and managers in differing degrees of work intensity. The differences in costs should be included in the cost-benefit analyses which compare the financial benefits of the various methods. The calculation of the cost price of labour carried out by internal employees (contractor, internal advisors, staff, secretariat) can be based on the costs estimate of an (internal) accounting service, for example. For employees on various scale levels an hourly rate can be calculated, based on costs arising from salary, pension, overhead, sickness and housing. Using this method, the real cost per hour of a staff member at academic level in a government job (corresponding to "salary scale 12" in the Netherlands), is estimated at 107 dollars.
  - Standpoint 3: Just as in standpoint 2 the cost price should be calculated. Direct cost price is not considered as the right

basis for the estimation. The line employee is not productive in his actual job during the hours that he/she is involved in an AC. The employee's turnover is often twice as much as the direct hourly cost. These so-called "opportunity costs" are clearly much higher than the direct cost price.

It is for the reader to decide which approach he/she opts for. However, the calculations that follow are based on the cost price model or the "no-cost" model.

Performance Costs

These include the following:

- *Assessor training courses*
  The cost of the advisor/trainer, and naturally that of the trainee assessors. Assessors generally have top level positions which makes the costs quite high.
- *Organisation of the AC*
  The cost of sending invitations, organising a location etc. Administration and P&O staff are often involved in this.
- *The performance of the AC*
  The cost of advisors, assessors and candidates is one of the largest expenses. Advisors often act as directors/coordinators. Sometimes role-players are used, but often advisors carry out this task. Finally, administrative and organisational support also falls under this category. They ensure that material is supplied and that coffee and lunch is served.
- *Reports and appraisal interviews*
  The advisor writes a report based on the information in the assessment scales. Then follows an interview in which candidates are given feedback on their performance. Assessors are often involved in this. Administrative support is also needed to process information and help with the production of the report.
- *Other costs*
  Costs incurred by the AC's location: the cost of travel, materials, the number and size of the rooms used in the AC, etc. Most organisations use external conference facilities. The cost of overnight accommodation is also taken into account if the AC takes more than one day.

Costs of Quality Control and Evaluation

In order to assess the effectiveness of an AC and make the necessary alterations, research has to be carried out. It is best to write this expense under a separate category. As in the case of development costs, these expenses can be written off over a long period of time and spread over various candidates. Quality control consists not only of gathering data for research into the predictive value of an AC (validity test), but may also involve research into the (psychometric) quality of the assessments or research into the experiences of the candidates and assessors. Investment in research is worthwhile because research provides insights into how one can make an AC more effective. Furthermore, contractors and candidates may ask, quite justifiably, for proof of an AC's effectiveness.

Calculation of the Cost per Candidate at Cost Price

Table 14.1 contains the previously mentioned cost categories. With the use of a spreadsheet it is very easy to calculate the costs of all types and sizes of ACs. This type of table also makes it easier to decide whether or not to hire a bureau.

Table 14.1 is based on an AC for upper management. The AC consists of three practical assignments. It lasts one and a half days and involves six candidates and six assessors. Candidates consist of employees working on an academic level with interest in management and the assessors are employed in upper management. The AC is used for selection and career advice. An external advice bureau, known as the Selection Centre, takes care of development, coordination, administration and quality control. The breakdown of costs is based on the assumption that the AC will be carried out at least 20 times with at least 120 candidates in total. After this, it will be necessary to develop new assignments.

The table is used to calculate the direct costs of assessors and candidates, as well as the price per candidate based on the "no cost" model.

The calculation of the cost of assessors and candidates is based on actual hourly rates, which were estimated by an internal accounting department, and not based on "opportunity costs".

Table 14.2 is based on the cost rundown shown in Table 14.1. It shows the relationship between the various cost categories

Table 14.1 Rundown of the costs involved in an Assessment Centre ("scale" refers to the government salary system for public personnel in the Netherlands)

	Assessor scale 15 $139 per hr	Candidate scale 13 $117 per hr	Advisors scale 13 $117 per hr	Administr. scale 5 $57 per hr	Total
AC development					
Scheme, methodology, develop assignments	200 hrs $27,800		400 hrs $46,800	80 hrs $4,560	680 hrs $79,160
Develop training programme for assessors			80 hrs $9,360		80 hrs $9,360
Other costs: materials, travel/ accommodation etc	p.m.		p.m.	p.m.	
Subtotal: development	200 hrs $27,800		480 hrs $56,160	80 hrs $4,560	760 hrs $88,520
AC performance (x20)					
Assessor training (2 days, 6 assessors)	96 hrs $13,344		32 hrs $3,744	8hrs $456	136 hrs $17,544
Practical organisation AC (20 x AC = 120 cand.)			80 hrs $9,360	320 hrs $18,240	400 hrs $27,600
Performance of AC programme (20 x AC = 120 cand)	1,440 hrs $200,160	960 hrs $112,320	320 hrs 37,440	160 hrs $9,120	2,880 hrs $359,040
Report + appraisal interviews with 120 candidates		240 hrs $28,080	480 hrs $56,160	160 hrs $9,120	880 hrs $93,360
Other costs: materials, travel/ accom./actors	p.m.	p.m.	p.m.	p.m.	p.m.
Evaluation, quality control (20 x AC)			40 hrs $4,680	40 hrs $2,280	80 hrs $6,960
Subtotal: AC Performance (20 x AC = 120 cand.)	1,536 hrs $213,504	1,200 hrs $140,400	952 hrs $111,384	688 hrs $39,216	4,376 hrs $504,504
TOTAL: development/ performance/ evaluation (per 120 candidates)	1,832 hrs $241,304	1,200 hrs $140,400	1,464 hrs $167,544	776 hrs $43,776	5,272 hrs $593,024
TOTAL: development/ performance/ evaluation (per 1 candidate)	15 hrs $2,011	10 hrs $1,170	12 hrs $1,357	6 hrs $365	44 hrs $4,942

Table 14.2 Costs of an AC per participant (costs for development, training and quality control and spread over 20 AC programmes with a total of 120 participants)

	Development	Training	Performance	Quality control	TOTAL
Candidate			$1,170 24%		$1,170 24%
Assessors	$232 5%	$111 2%	$1,668 34%		$2,011 41%
Advisors	$168 9%	$31 1%	$858 17%	$39 1%	$1,396 28%
Administration	$38 1%	$4 0%	$304 6%	$19 0%	$365 7%
Other	p.m.	p.m.	p.m.	p.m.	p.m.
TOTAL	$738 15%	$146 3%	$4,363 81%	$58 1%	$4,942 100%

and the cost per group of participants. The greatest proportion (81%) of the costs are incurred by the actual AC. The development costs make up 15% of the total cost, spread over 120 participants.

These figures are based on an AC that was developed and carried out by the same organisation. They decided to carry out 20 AC programmes including 120 candidates. In this way high development costs were reduced to an acceptable level by proportional debiting. When deciding whether to contract a bureau or not, it is important to realise that the cost of internal assessors and internal candidates during the actual performance of the AC, take up a high proportion of the total costs. These type of costs still have to be paid even if an organisation opts for an external bureau. In the event of external candidates, however, a proportion of the costs is withheld.

If an organisation maintains that advisors and candidates should regard their work in an AC as part of their everyday duties (no costs model), then the cost of an AC is reduced by $3,181 (64%) to $1,761.

14.5 THE FINANCIAL RETURNS OF AN ASSESSMENT CENTRE

Factors in the Utility Model

The utility model of Brogden, Cronbach and Gleser is designed to calculate the added returns of selection procedures and provides an answer to the following question:

"If we compare an employee who was selected by an AC with an employee selected by conventional procedures, how much more money is he/she worth, in terms of productivity and the services that he/she provides?"

The previous sections of this chapter dealt with the validity and costs of the AC in relation to its financial returns; the following sections deal with other factors that influence this.

Standard Dollar Deviation (SDD)

AC candidates aspire to a job in a company. A certain turnover expectation is attached to the job. The greater the turnover expectation the higher the value of the job for the company and the higher the damage to the candidate who fails. The value of the job can usually be determined by the salary. SDD is a system of measurement related to the value of a job or the risk of damage that it entails.

Organisations are well aware of the fact that performance level differs from person to person. The productivity of employees is normally distributed, on the whole. It is necessary to find out how employees perform their job, and their differences in terms of productivity. The difference is expressed in dollars. Research indicates that SDD can be calculated by subtracting the annual salary by 40%. If the annual salary is $120,000 the SDD is worked out as 0.40 x 120,000 = $48,000.

Selection Ratio (SR)

Organisations usually appoint employees by choosing someone from a group of applicants. For example: five candidates apply for the same job. All five of them are assessed in an AC. The candidate with the best results gets the job. The selection ratio is the relationship between the number of vacancies and the number of candidates. In this example the SR is 1/5 or 0.20.

Validity and the Cost of Alternative Procedures

In order to calculate the returns of an AC in comparison with traditional methods, we have to determine the validity and costs per candidate of the traditional procedure.

Application of the Utility Model

As a formula the utility model is expressed as follows:

Added utility = (R2 – R1) . (SDD) . M – (C2 – C1)/SR

R2 = the validity of the new method
R1 = the validity of the old method
C2 = the cost of the new method
C1 = the cost of the old method
M = the average score of candidates in the selection procedure. This is related to the selection ratio (SR)

The first part of the formula is related to the difference in benefits and the second part is related to the difference in costs.

Using this formula we can calculate the added returns of an AC compared to an interview. For this calculation we will use the following amounts:

SDD = $48,000 (standard dollar deviation)
SR   = 0.20 (selection ratio)
C1   = $1,000 (cost of the interview)
R1   = 0.25 (validity of the interview)

For C2 (cost of the AC) we fill in two amounts: $4,942 ("cost price" model) and $1,761 ("no cost" model). We use two amounts for R2 (validity of the AC): 0.37 (criterion: performance) and 0.53 (criterion: assessment of potential).

Using this formula for an AC costing $19,710 for the amounts of R2 = 0.37 and C2 = 4992 for the selection of one candidate from a group of five (SR = 0.2), the AC is calculated as being more expensive than an interview. The annual returns of an AC are, however, $8,063 – more than the interview. In other words, due to the higher validity of the AC, the employee who was selected by this method would be more profitable than the employee who was selected by traditional methods. Initially, it might seem as though the AC involved a loss of $11,647. One should take into account that the cost of selection is one-off, whereas profits come in year after year. If the employee stays with the company for three years, then the AC is more profitable than the interview. If the employee stays for five years the added returns of the AC is $20,605 [(5 x $8063) – $19,710]. If the employee stays for 10 years the added returns of the AC over this period are $60,920. The added returns are directly proportional to the number of people employed by the organisation. If 20

Table 14.3 Income, costs and returns per year (in $), of an employee with an employment term of five years, who was selected by an AC with validities of 0.37 and 0.53 and costing $4,932 and $1,761.

	Income	Costs	Returns	Returns over 5 years
$R_2 = 0.37$ $C_2 = 4,942$	8,063	19,710	–11,647	20,605
$R_2 = 0.37$ $C_2 = 1,761$	8,063	3,805	4,258	36,510
$R_2 = 0.53$ $C_2 = 4,942$	18,815	19,710	–895	74,365
$R_2 = 0.53$ $C_2 = 1,761$	18,815	3,805	15,010	90,270

people are employed via an AC per year, the added returns of selection will increase by a factor of 20.

Table 14.3 shows that the AC's returns are closely related to:

1. the validity that one postulates;
2. the way in which one deals with the cost of the assessors and the candidates. If we take a higher validity ($R2= 0.53$) and a low price ($C2 = \$1,761$) then the returns are more than four times as high.

For purposes of illustration, we can use this model to compare the returns of an AC with those of throwing dice. Throwing dice does not cost anything ($C1 = 0$), but is also not valid ($R1 = 0$). If we use the same figures, the AC will cost $25,000 more than throwing dice. The annual returns of an AC instead of dice is $24,862. For an employment term of one year or less it is better to choose someone by throwing dice. After 5 or 10 years of service, the employee will bring in an added return of $99,310 and $223,620 respectively.

ACs are often the last stage in a series of selection procedures. Organisations usually start by conducting a series of interviews with applicants and then invite the most promising candidates to take part in an AC, after which they make their final choice. With a few adaptations, the utility model can be used to calculate to what extent the multi phase procedure is better than, for example, an interview. The result of this calculation, which is not included here, shows that the added returns of a multi-phase procedure can be higher than that of a single interview or AC. Based on an employment term of five years, a multi-phase procedure in which candidates are selected by an interview and an AC, can result in at least $30,000 more than the use of a single interview and $8,000 more than a single AC.

There are some criticisms of this model. The model is based on the assumption that candidates with the highest scores will accept the job. However, this is not always the case. Sometimes candidates refuse the job offer and accept a job elsewhere. At other times the organisation might opt for someone else. Moreover, in purely business terms, when calculating the added returns, it is probably more logical to take into account the returns that the investment could have achieved elsewhere, on the capital market, for example. On the other hand, the model overlooks the other areas in which the AC can be profitable.

The model clearly shows that it is not very businesslike to consider the cost of a selection procedure in isolation from other factors. It shows that a relatively expensive method like the AC can be a profitable alternative to, what may on the surface appear to be, cheaper methods of selection.

14.6 PROFITABLE SPIN-OFFS

The AC has a number of beneficial spin-offs that are not shown in the utility model.

1. Participation in an AC by internal assessors encourages more commitment to assessment and selection than any other method. This is related to the factors that were discussed in the introduction.
2. Managers improve their skills in this area and apply them in their day to day work.
3. They learn more effective means of communication.
4. They learn how to observe more keenly and are supplied with methods which help them to give feedback more efficiently.
5. The process of writing AC reports makes managers better equipped to conduct career interviews.
6. ACs can save on expenses. Due to the practical nature of assignments, candidates become familiar with the organisation and the job that they are applying for, which means that less time is needed in preparing the successful candidate for the job.

REFERENCES

Brogden, H.E. (1949), When Testing Pays Off, *Personnel Psychology*, **2** 171–185.
Cronbach, L.T. and Gleser, G.C. (1965), *Psychological tests and personnel decisions*, 2nd ed., Urbana, Illinois: University of Illinois Press.
Gangler, B.B. *et al.* (1987), Meta-analysis of assessment center validity, *Journal of Applied Psychology*, **72**, 493–511.
Klimoski, R., and Brickner, M. (1987), Why do assessment centers work? The puzzle of assessment center validity, *Personnel Psychology*, **40**, 243–260.
Moses, J.L. and Byham, W.C. (eds) (1977), *Applying the assessment-center method*, New York: Pergamon Press.

_____ Chapter 15

Assessment Centres and Management Development

E.L. Steltenpöhl

15.1 INTRODUCTION

The role of management development can be described as making sure that the ambitions and potential of employees are compatible with the demands of the organisation that they work for. Management development works with two different sources of information: that of the individual and that of the organisation. It is difficult to combine these sources. This often results in essential information being unavailable at times when it is most needed, during selection, for example. In this way it is impossible to find the perfect match between employee and vacancy.

Once the vacancy has been filled, some people may complain of being badly informed during the selection procedure. This will lead to misunderstandings and frustration between employers and employees, and ultimately undermine their faith in MD activities. Also, management wants absolute certainty, especially during selection. If MD cannot provide this type of

Assessment Centres: A Practical Handbook, P. Jansen and F. de Jongh.
© 1997 John Wiley & Sons Ltd.

certainty, management will take the matter into their own hands, and refer to their own sources of information. This often results in them appointing someone from their own coterie.

MD should focus upon the process of developing management. Instead of this it tends to be more preoccupied with administration, concentrating on instrumental aspects such as evaluation systems, career courses and career policies geared towards the so-called "high potentials". Social developments such as individualisation, economic uncertainties and the use of new technologies have made MD activities more complicated. The more traditional MD approach regards changes in employee potential (in their interests or needs) as "limitations". In the same way, they regard changes in organisations and their expectations as "problematical".

This chapter deals with the crucial role that Assessment Centres can play in solving these, and other, MD problems. The complex nature of today's organisations demands a different MD approach and different MD instruments. The AC method can offer an effective response to this new demand.

15.2   COHERENCE

Successful management development requires more than having systems like job classification and performance evaluation at one's disposal. The quality of these separate systems is important, but it is far more important that they cohere with one another. It is the lack of cohesion that makes the use of different instruments and procedures ineffective. It has nothing to do with the separate instruments or procedures or the manager, or his qualifications, input or intentions.

The AC method makes the cohesion between different systems possible, as well as providing a good basis for communication about the outcomes of MD projects.

15.3   INSTRUMENTS

MD has built up a lot of experience working with instruments for job classification, which uses specific criteria to determine where a job should be placed on the salary scale. This system establishes a relationship between the tasks, or aim, of the organisation, and the individual salaries given to employees. It is essential that the job evaluation and remuneration systems have a high level of mutual cohesion and consistency. This makes the outcomes clear and renders effective communication between organisations and employees possible, even when there are conflicts about actual job descriptions and salaries.

The same type of criteria should also be applied to MD activities that deal with qualifications. In this case, a means of communication should be found that brings the job requirements into perspective but also allows candidates to talk about their capacities. The criteria that are used in the AC method are perfect for this outcome. It is essential that the criteria that are used in ACs complement with other systems of management development and vice versa. The use of ACs demands careful consideration of existing systems and more importantly, cohesion with these systems. What type of place should ACs have in MD? Should they be fully integrated or regarded as separate systems? When ACs are used as separate systems, they still involve large investments, but do give organisations less guarantees of visible results in the daily practices of management development.

15.4   THE INFORMATIVE TASK OF MD IN RELATION TO THE AC

Before the selection procedure is started, it is essential to gather information that is relevant to the vacancy. This information should be objective, and relevant to the recruitment and selection procedure, as well as the candidate's future development so that it can be used for future MD activities.

The "lifetime employment" concept, which assumed that employees would remain with a company for the rest of their working lives, is no longer prevalent. Economic circumstances; many companies can no longer offer lifetime employment guarantees, and social developments (balance between work and pleasure), encourage many employees to strive for maximum employability. This could be described as a shift from "lifetime employment" to "lifetime enjoyment". This shift in emphasis has made it more important for employees to be well informed so that they can plan their future careers. The question of where one works has become less relevant; it is far more important for personal ambitions to be fulfilled. If an organisation does not keep its employees well informed, it may risk losing employees or, even worse perhaps, giving them false hopes.

ACs supply information on someone's current capacities and future potential (within the existing organisation or elsewhere), which allows organisations to construct development plans that conform with individual potential. More importantly, ACs provide reliable information that can be used in MD activities.

15.5   THE ROLE OF MD AND MANAGEMENT IN ACs

Managers play a key role in ACs. They are involved in job analysis, determining the criteria on which candidates are tested and the actual methods of evaluation. Furthermore, some managers work as assessors during the AC and conduct feedback interviews.

Management plays a central role in the AC, but what does the MD function contribute? They act as professional counsellors and quality controllers, ensuring that managers work to the best of their ability. Furthermore, MD makes sure that AC participants are well informed and that obligations are fulfilled. Most importantly, management development has the task of supervising the AC and making sure that the results are used professionally and honestly.

15.6   STRUCTURE, PROCESSES AND THE ROLE OF ACs

"Flow-in"

The "flow-in", the moment when a new employee joins an organisation, is a decisive moment for the organisation and the employee. If the organisation in which the candidate seeks employment is widely different from the organisation in which the candidate is employed, there is a greater need to test whether the transfer will be successful or not. Obviously, companies have more information on internal candidates, but this is no guarantee for a better choice. Sometimes internal information is biased, or leans too much towards the individual or the company which only adds to MD's workload.

Most mistakes occur during this first stage of selection. Therefore there is a growing need for a more effective and reliable method of selection – one that is based on the specific needs of the organisation and not on the actual vacancy. This shift in emphasis will lead to a better understanding of the factors that are critical for an organisation's success. Managers have the job of indicating which factors are critical. This gives them more insight into the type of role that jobs should play within the organisation. In this way they learn how to look at vacancies in a different light. Finally, in relation to job requirements, one should ask which criteria are crucial to the vacancy and investigate whether the candidate can fulfil these criteria or not. Here we touch upon the very essence of ACs.

ACs put high demands on organisations long before any results are booked, forcing organisations to think carefully about key processes and key activities. It is pointless to select candidates without a clear idea of the type of criteria that are crucial to their place within an organisation. Determining criteria via an AC is the best way of ensuring a suitable match between organisation and individual.

"Flow-through"

The missing link in many MD systems and procedures is a follow-up to the AC. Once a candidate is appointed the candidate is subject to the regular evaluation procedures. This should not present any problems, if the procedures and systems of internal and external selection conform with one another, but often this is not the case. Many organisations that use ACs for external selection do not apply the AC method to internal selection. In this way valuable information is lost and a double standard is created. This may also cause employees who were selected by ACs, to doubt whether such a rigorous procedure was necessary, whereas existing employees (internal candidates) may wonder why they never received much attention.

The AC is an ideal system for following an employee's progress within an organisation and determining development plans. ACs can also be used as supplements to applied evaluation systems. Employees who have reached a certain level through promotion, can be assessed in an AC on their suitability for higher functions. In this way the AC can serve as a reference point for the type of qualities required for upper management levels.

Systematic use of ACs is effective in keeping top management, in the role of assessors, in close contact with potential top managers. One of the greatest dilemmas for top management is to determine whether employees who always score highly in assessments are suitable for top positions. ACs are designed to assess candidates' potential and compare their results. As for employees, ACs serve as a link between current and future functions. Clear and constructive feedback enables them to take action in the necessary areas.

"Flow-out"

More and more organisations recognise the need to adopt a more open attitude to outside influences, and use external candidates to improve their strength on all levels. Outside competition also demands a certain level of openness and flexibility within organisations. Organisations that use internal candidates for top management vacancies build up a tightknit culture, but this can be counterproductive and result in over-competitiveness. Another reason for the increase in external recruitment is due to the lack of affinity that employees feel for their organisation, which can lead to an increase in the flow-out of employees. If this is tackled well, both trends (flow-in and flow-out) offer new possibilities for internal promotion and external recruitment. Activities directed towards "flow-out" (different to, for example, outplacement) are still very limited. ACs and their outcomes provide employees with realistic perspectives. They start discussions about individual expectations set against those of the organisation. It is less threatening to the employee if these types of discussion take place immediately after the AC.

15.7 MANAGEMENT DEVELOPMENT AND ITS INTERESTED PARTIES

Management Commitment and ACs

What type of role does management play in management development activities? Management development is often criticised for excluding Management from their activities, whereas MD accuses Management of being one-sided, and evading responsibility. Not surprisingly, both parties regard each other's activities with suspicion.

This is where ACs prove their worth. Their success is due to the type of approach they use – an approach based on the organisation's needs. Once the organisations needs are determined, managers translate these needs into the most relevant criteria. In this way, a firm basis is established for assessment and selection. ACs increase management commitment. During traditional selection procedures, managers are committed to securing the most appealing candidate. In ACs, however, managers are committed to an integral process. They are committed to the criteria on which the candidates are assessed, to the procedures that they follow and to the AC's final outcome. The fact that this result is achieved by logical stages also increases commitment.

What distinguishes ACs most from more traditional methods of selection is the importance that they lend to the contents of the selection process. Managers are concerned with questions like "What have I observed? What have other managers observed? To what extent did candidates fulfil the criteria?". ACs should not only be seen as instruments of selection but also as effective communicators, in terms of the information that they supply on behaviour criteria, performance in assignments and candidates' results.

Organisational Development

Management development attempts to improve organisations by developing their management using career models. They give some indication of the type of career courses available to managers and list the type of functions managers should expect, their order of succession and the type of training that they would require. The interface of career models with the specific demands and expectations of organisations is often a source of many problems.

AC outcomes can also be used to examine how well an organisation is constructed. Organisational development requires clear information that can be translated into concrete action. Communication plays an essential role in this. The MD employee may ask: "How can I make top management aware of Human Resources' strengths and weaknesses?" Top management may struggle with a similar problem: "Which areas are weak? Which areas of management are at risk? How can we test our strategies on current and future possibilities? How can we control these aspects?". Organisations spend a great deal of time making decisions about primary salary costs or training budgets, but rather surprisingly, do not have essential information at their disposal, ie analyses on the quality of an organisation, possible lines of improvement, the investments involved in this and the eventual returns. If ACs are used consistently within organisations, this type of information is produced as a matter of course and put at the disposal of upper management and MD. This will give rise to a discussion on macro level, about the quality and construction of Human Resources, set against the organisation's long- and short-term needs. In this way, the short-term policies that are used in filling vacancies are placed in a larger context; maintaining the right qualitative and quantative levels within the workforce.

Other Implications

Generally speaking, ACs will only be considered worthwhile if they have more value than other selection procedures (see Chapter 14). This extra value should be seen in terms of the relationship between investment and visible returns. Two parties are involved in selection: the organisation (for example the head of Management Development and a manager) and the candidates. Compared to other selection procedures, the AC method demands a high level of involvement from managers. They are expected to supply information, take part in the construction of the AC, and work as assessors. Most managers have to train for this.

From the point of view of the candidate, the difference between ACs and traditional procedures is quite considerable. ACs are far more intensive and, unlike interviews, leave candidates no room to guide the course of the proceedings. Since ACs are more rigorous, candidates are no longer satisfied with short letters of rejection, but expect detailed information on their performance. In this way, even candidates regard ACs in terms of investment and returns.

The Surplus Value of ACs in MD

ACs are expensive, generate high expectations and put explicit demands on managers and MD employees. But do they create enough surplus value? Since ACs are more effective than other MD instruments, the surplus value should be related to the candidates as well as management and MD professionals.

The introduction of the AC method in an organisation can be seen as an intervention in the area of personnel policies and data resources. ACs provide employees with information on the demands and expectations of the organisation, and organisations with information on the current and future capacities of Human Resources. The structural use of ACs does not tolerate any ambiguity between organisations and employees. This often involves changes in personnel policies and staff reorganisations. Staff reorganisations and the extra tasks and responsibilities that the AC would involve, makes one suspect that ACs will not be introduced into organisations as a matter of course, indeed managers and employees are often strongly opposed to their introduction.

Consistent use of ACs provides employees with information that can help them plan realistic career strategies. ACs provoke thought. This effect alone will lead to improvements in employee development and their value to the organisation. If ACs are combined with a policy-based management approach (management will be in the position of determining more quickly and accurately what type of capacities and ambitions employees have), they will lead to improvements in HR. ACs will generate the highest surplus value if they are used as an integral part of the organisation. Peripheral use of ACs has negative implications for MD. When the AC is in use, MD employees have the authority to inform managers of their responsibility to HR. When ACs are not in use, however, their role becomes rather vague.

What type of effect does the *ad hoc* use of ACs have on individual employees? Do they produce better results, or a higher level of acceptance? Even if ACs are only used for a select group, eg academics, there are some doubts as to whether the results justify the means. If no follow-up action is provided or no further use is made of the information supplied by the AC, the person who was selected in this way may doubt the validity of the method. On the other hand, employees who did not participate in an AC may wonder why they were not selected in this way. ACs have the highest surplus value if they are *fully* integrated with the other instruments and systems within MD. This surplus value should not only be related to ACs and their results but also to other systems.

Finally, ACs place high demands on MD professionals. ACs require MD employees to have in-depth knowledge of the organisation, its construction, its key processes, its business strategies, and external influences on these strategies. ACs leave no room for departmental politics, but involve MD in a role that extends far further than reporting on personnel issues. During ACs, MD professionals are expected to communicate on an equal level with top management. This means that they need more expertise and business experience. Any doubts about the justification of MD should be resolved by the type of participation that ACs expect from them. ACs upgrade MD, so that they are no longer engaged in merely striving for a result but actually achieving it. In this way, MD takes on a different dimension (curtailment) and is put in the right relationship to line management.

FURTHER READING

Ballantyne, I. and Povah, N. (1995). *Assessment & development centres*, Gower Publishing, Aldershot.
(A comprehensive book for students and practitioners looking at the entire process, from concepts to validation methods and organisational politics.)

Woodruffe, C. (1993). *Assessment centres: Identifying and developing competence (2nd ed.)*, Institute of Personnel Management, London.
(Updated and expanded version of the original practitioner text, published in 1990, with emphasis upon developing and designing ACs.)

ABOUT THE AUTHORS

Katinka Geling works as a trainer for Smits & Partners in Groningen, the Netherlands.

Mark de Graaff is a co-founder and co-director of Assessment Development Consult in Arnhem, the Netherlands.

Dr Paul Jansen is Professor of Industrial Psychology at the Department of Business Administration, Faculty of Economics and Econometrics, of the Free University of Amsterdam, the Netherlands.

Ferry de Jongh is a senior consultant at Briar Hill Consult in Zoetermeer, the Netherlands.

Paul F. van Leest is a senior consultant at Briar Hill Consult in Zoetermeer, the Netherlands.

Dr Paul van der Maesen de Sombreff is Senior Lecturer at the University of Tilburg, Department Human Resource Science, and a part-time consultant.

Cora Reijerse is a senior consultant at ACT, the Netherlands.

Jeroen Seegers is a co-founder and co-director of Assessment Development Consult in Arnhem, the Netherlands.

Ernst Steltenpöhl is a Human Resources consultant manager at LTP in Amsterdam, the Netherlands.

J. de Veer is Head of Research at the Inland Revenue's Selection Centre in the Netherlands.

The late Willem Vogtschmit was a senior consultant at LTP in Amsterdam, the Netherlands.

INDEX